The Religion of Socialism by Ernest Belfort Bax
2011 Prism Key Press | www.prismkeypress.com

# The Religion of Socialism
# Socialism
Ernest Belfort Bax

# Contents

Preface................................................................................7
Universal History from a Socialist Standpoint ..................13
A French Economist on Collectivism ...............................45
Socialism and Religion.....................................................54
Socialism and the Sunday Question...................................60
Conscience and Commerce................................................65
Unscientific Socialism......................................................73
The Criminal Court Judge.................................................86
Some Bourgeois Idols; Or Ideals, Reals, and Shams..........91
Imperialism v. Socialism.................................................102
The Two Enthusiasms......................................................106
The Commercial Hearth...................................................113
Civil Law under Socialism..............................................123
Appendix.........................................................................131

# Preface

A FEW introductory words may seem necessary in presenting the following pieces to the public in book-form. They have most of them already appeared in various periodicals (*Time, To-day, Commonweal, Justice*, etc.), and this fact will explain any repetition of idea or mode of statement which may here and there be discoverable, also their, to some extent, heterogeneous character.

The first article contains a condensed presentation of the cardinal points in the evolution of history. Such a statement must necessarily pass over many important details, and leave little room for illustration. The chief aim here has been to enforce the truth that the evolution of human society is a progress from Socialism to Socialism – from the simple, limited, tribal Socialism of early man to the complex universal Socialism already prepared in the womb of time. The treatment of this vast theme at a length which will admit of its approximately adequate discussion in all its bearings, is a task the author hopes to accomplish in the future; but at present the following brief instalment was all that could be given.

Other essays in the present volume touch upon the same subject directly or indirectly. It cannot be too strongly insisted upon that either the theory of modern Socialism rests on a solid historical basis, or it is nothing. The truth discovered by Marx, that the basal factor determining the constitution of society is its material and economic condition, must be for the Socialist the key to the reconstruction of history. Socialism, we contend, is not a theory "won from the void and formless infinite" of Utopian sentiment and good intentions, very beautiful, but impracticable,

7

as some think; or from that of an aimless discontent acted on by wicked and designing agitators, as others think; but it is a plain deduction from the facts of history. The living form of Socialism has been long perfecting itself within the chrysalis of Civilisation. The process completed, nothing will prevent the dried hull from bursting asunder and the new being from issuing forth in its fairness and freedom. The more repulsive, the more dead and withered, the harder in outline the forms of Civilisation appear, the sooner may we look for their final destruction. We often hear of the taunt from middle-class thinkers and writers, "I am no Revolutionist, I am an Evolutionist." This abstract way of looking at things is characteristic of current bourgeois habits of thought. To be an Evolutionist in the view of these gentlemen is tantamount to being an anti-Revolutionist. The notion of Evolution is erected into an absolute category, which is supposed to embrace the sum total of all sweet reasonableness in social matters. Over against this is another opposing category, – that of Revolution. Just as Evolution is the sum total in bourgeois eyes of all possible rationality, so Revolution is the sum total from the same point of view of all possible irrationality, – Ormuszd and Arhiman, the kingdom of light and the kingdom of darkness. But the scientific Socialist who takes a concrete view of things, unhampered by the abstractions in which the current thinker is immersed, fails to discover in the real world any revolution that is not part of evolution, or any evolution that excludes the possibility of revolution as one of its moments.

The inability of the middle-class intellect to view things otherwise than abstractly is not surprising seeing that our whole bourgeois civilisation is a system of abstractions erected into independent existences. In evidence of this we have only to look at the existence of classes itself; each class being simply in the last resort an embodied abstraction. Thus, out, of the distinction between the social functions of direction and immediate production have arisen the embodied abstractions of an upper,

8

possessing, and ruling class, and a lower, non-possessing, and ruled class, within which moulds the conflict between individual interests as such, over social interests has worked itself out, to the temporary victory of the former. So with the subordinate classes within these classes, each one is the embodiment of some phase of human life, torn or abstracted from the rest, that is, from the whole to which it belongs. The same with our culture. In the specialisation which characterises the learning of the nineteenth century, the basal unity of knowledge is lost sight of, and each little grovelling specialist thinks that in his own science and its methods the fulness of knowledge is manifested. He despises philosophy, one function of which is to reduce his speciality to a mere aspect of a larger whole. His science is his philosophy, much in the same way as the "public" of the ordinary man is his class.

The progress of the capitalistic system has tended to render the economic bedrock of all things social, increasingly evident, by reducing the super-incumbent strata to a more and more rudimentary condition. Hence the anachronistic absurdity of Conservatism. We are not here referring merely to current politics, the rival parties of which are only too obviously of the nature of business firms who trade in the emoluments of office; but to the underlying principle which Conservatism may be supposed to have originally embodied. On the face of it Conservatism meant the desire of the decaying feudal or landed class to maintain itself against the rising middle or capitalist class. But in addition to this primary question of class interest, it is certain there was in many minds a genuine horror at the vulgarisation of life and the destruction of old-world sentiment and institutions which they instinctively felt the ascendency of the capitalist class to involve. Some had also, doubtless, a glimmering of the truth that "progress" in the middle-class sense did not mean a material betterment for the mass of the people, but rather the reverse. Such we may suppose to have been the

9

sentiment which underlay (in some cases at least) the Conservatism of the Royalist side during the English parliamentary struggle of the seventeenth century.

But the work of destruction has now been done. There is no longer anything to conserve in the old sense. The aristocratic or landed classes of to-day are simply a wing of the "great middle class" in every sense of the word. Land itself is, in the present day, simply one of the forms of fined capital. The landlord's sole aim is to obtain the greatest amount of surplus value in the form of rent from his land. The reciprocal duties of the medieval lord and tenant, their religious sanctions, and the sentiment they involved, have passed away absolutely and completely. The lord himself is more often than not a trader; he invests the unconsumed portion of his revenue in some business enterprise, and is invariably a shareholder in joint-stock companies, even when he is not a promoter or director of the same. As such his sympathies are as much with "improvements" in machinery, with the extension of railways, the opening-up of the world-market, and the spread of bourgeois civilisation generally, as the middle-class parvenu himself. It becomes more and more evident that we have to-day but two classes in society, – the capitalist class and the working class. The House of Lords is simply a legislative body of capitalists possessed of a special monopoly. The plea which the Conservative of old had is, therefore, no longer valid. All that is now to be conserved are the very things which to the Conservatism of the past were the abomination of desolation. The past, that might have been conceived, in a sense, as worth preserving, has already disappeared, save for some tattered rags, befouled with the filth of a world in which they are an anachronism and an absurdity, and about the continuance of which no one really cares. The true Conservative is, therefore, of necessity as extinct as the dodo; and the modern political Conservative is simply a "Liberal," or, in other words, an upholder of the modern capitalistic order, trading under another name. It is necessary to point out these things, as there are occasionally to be found Rip van Winkles, who, while bitterly hostile to middle-class Philistinism in all its aspects, yet persist in calling themselves Conservative. The Rip-van-Winkleism in question is, however, it is to be feared, too often no more than a piece of silly affectation and bizarrerie.

Socialism is the great, modern protest against unreality, against the delusive shams which now masquerade as verities. It has this at least, if nothing else, in common with primitive Christianity. Early Christianity affirmed that principle of absolute morality, of individualism, of the mystical relation of the soul to the supernatural, as the basis of religion, which represented the real intellectual tendencies and aspirations of the period, in opposition to the established but unreal state-religion of the Roman Empire, representing, as it did, the forms of things which had ceased to be, viz., the old race-solidarity in communal and city life, and the naive conception of nature as directly personified. Similarly, Socialists to-day affirm the principle of human solidarity through the triumph of the cause of labour, i.e., the real interest of the modern world against the bourgeois civilisation that professes to represent an economic individualism which has ceased to be; and against its ethical and speculative counterpart, the introspection and supernaturalism, which have also ceased be as living realities. The great industry has destroyed the last vestige of the one; science (using the word in its widest sense) has destroyed the last vestige of the other. But in both cases the dead forms remain. The bourgeois moralist is never tired of preaching the reform of the individual character as the first condition of human happiness, ignoring the fact, that science knows of no such thing as an individual character, apart from social surroundings. He holds fast the old fallacious standpoint, according to which individual good men make healthy social conditions, rather than acknowledge the truth that it is healthy social conditions which make good men; in the same way that it

11

is not great men which make history, but (as is recognised by every critical student of history in the present clay) that it is history which makes great men. The old supernaturalist creeds drag on their meaningless existence. Men are classed as Catholics and Protestants, Christians and Moslems, quite irrespective of their real beliefs. By the conditions of their livelihood they are bound to let it be supposed that they give their adhesion to doctrines respecting which they have not given an hour's thought in their lives, or which they may actually despise in their hearts.

Socialism breaks through these shams, in protesting that no amount of determination on the part of the individual to regenerate himself, however successful he may be in cultivating the correct ethical trim, will of itself affect in aught the welfare of society; that concern for the social whole is the one object of religion; and that the placing above this of any abstract theological ideal, be it Christian, Mussulman, or Buddhist is (to employ the old phraseology) an act of apostacy. On this view the old theological questions, such as that of the continuance of the individual consciousness after death, may be interesting, but have no more ethical or religious importance than other interesting questions, such as that of the origin of the irregular Greek verbs, or of the personal or impersonal authorship of the Homeric poems.

In concluding (with apologies to the reader for having been seduced into extending what should have been an orthodox preface into something like an independent disquisition on Socialism), I will venture to express the hope that the present little volume may, notwithstanding the somewhat promiscuous nature of its contents, be not entirely without suggestiveness to those for whom Modern Socialism has an interest.

# Universal History from a Socialist Standpoint

From The Religion of Socialism, pp.1-37.

"All things flow," said Herakleitos of Ephesus. Translated into modern language this is as much as to say, "The reality of any given thing is simply the temporary form assumed by the elements composing it." In the historical development of the world we find stretched out, on (if we may so speak) the procrustean bed of time, the different factors which go to make up our life and civilisation of to-day, no less than that of any other period on which we may choose to fix our attention. Every custom, every law, every religious belief or rite, our very thought, language, characters, habits, not to speak of our architecture, our clothing, our literature, which are their outward and visible expression, could, both severally and as a whole, be traced back and back into the night of the past, till lost in prehistoric times and primitive forms of social life. All this may sound familiar enough, and some may even be disposed to resent the statement of it as a platitude. Yet how few really grasp the great truth, that they and theirs, as they appear to-day, are but products of a long historic development. How little do they realise that, were they to go but a short way back into the past, they would cease to recognise the characteristics of modern society; that their most cherished beliefs and practices, perchance, might be found to take their origin from such as would excite their keenest horror and indignation! How little do they dream that their conceptions of history, of past periods of civilisation, even when they have any, are unconsciously coloured through and through by the world they see around them? The critical conception of history, for which history is a succession of dependent social formations, one born from the other; in short, the true notion of human development as a continuity in diversity is perhaps the most important and wide-reaching speculative truth to which the nineteenth century has given birth. Once we occupy the critical standpoint, and we see history in a new light; then, for the first time, we discern a meaning in the often apparently capricious course of historic events. (See Appendix, I)

The method of historical sequence is based on that of logical sequence, but with the difference, that the abstract logical movement, as realised on the plane of history, has to be discovered by analysis and disentangled, so to speak, in its several lines, from the unessential matter with which it is encumbered. All growth or evolution involves the notion of capacity unrealised, and capacity realised; in the language of the schools, of the potential and the actual, of the matter and the form. The acorn is the unrealised capacity of the oak, which is realised in the oak; the new-born infant constitutes the capacity or possibility of the full-gown man; the capacity present in the child realises itself in the farm of the man. But the realisation of the capacity of a thing involves the destruction or negation of the immediate or present existence of that thing. Every step in the growth of a child is a step towards the negation of childhood. In proportion as the child progresses towards manhood the less he is of a child. In the man, the child, quâ child, no longer exists, any more than if he were dead. In the realisation of the perfection of the child's faculties his childhood is abolished. In the same way the oak-tree presupposes the negation of the acorn; the acorn, as acorn, wears itself out and breaks up; but the moment of the destruction of the acorn is the moment of the genesis of the oak. The same process is seen throughout all life.

It appears, then, that growth implies a process comprising

14

three terms; the first, indefinite and crude, with the seeds of its own negation present in it as part of its very nature from the first; the second, the accomplishment of this negation, which accomplishment, however, becomes the matrix whence issues the third and final term of the process, which is nothing else than the negation of that negation. Here what was latent capacity becomes reality; what was potential becomes actual; what was merely tendency becomes fact. But this Dialectic does not lie on the surface of history any more than on that of other planes of knowledge. The concrete world is a complex network of many different lines, each working out its own process; and in the entanglement of these lines it is sometimes difficult to discover the central course of development. As we have already pointed out, we are not here concerned with the logical process in its abstract and pure form. In history, as in the real world generally, it may be arrested, delayed, or modified in any particular instance, without any infringement of the general principle. A given seed, for instance, may die, or its vitality be suspended for years; or it may live and its normal development be diverted by some external cause. The aim and meaning of the philosophy of history- is the discovery of the Dialectic immanent in it, of the main process underlying the whole development. For in spite of the complexity which seems at first sight so insuperable, we can undoubtedly discern a main stream of development embodying itself, during one epoch, in one group of races or peoples, and passing on perhaps in the next epoch to another such ethnic group, but maintaining itself through the diversity of the material in which it is successively realised as the same stream of tendency, a movement one and indivisible. (See Appendix, II.) Thus, in history as elsewhere, nothing passes away absolutely, since all that has preceded forms an essential part of all that follows, a truth which, platitude as it may seem at first sight, can never be too assiduously borne in mind.

In the earliest period of human society man does not

15

distinguish himself from the natural forces and objects around him. He conceives of nature as like himself animated and conscious, and hence as capable of being friendly or unfriendly towards him. In this stage, also, the individual man, as an individual, has not consciously distinguished himself or his interests from those of his fellow-men with whom be is associated; in other words, he is completely identified with his social surroundings; he lives simply in and for the society which has produced him. In consequence, all life, all work, all enjoyment, all government, is in common; individual interests and individual property are unknown. The individual, in short, is completely merged in the race. This earliest condition of man as a social being is what is sometimes referred to as Primitive Communism. It is essentially the prehistoric era, in human development – that of the Lake dwellers of Switzerland, of the men of the drift, and of the countless apes which succeeded before chronology begins. Yet, although it is mainly prehistoric, and therefore only to be reconstructed in imagination from its surviving traces in various parts of the civilised world, or from the crude, imperfect analogy afforded by the savage and barbaric races of the present day, we find rich indications of it in the world's oldest literary monuments; in the Homeric poems, the Icelandic sagas, the Nibelungenlied, etc. As regards the surviving traces of its economical forms which we have spoken of, existing like little oases in the arid desert of civilisation surrounding them, we may refer by way of illustration to the Russian Mir, the Swiss Allemen, and the Hindoo village community, etc. How long this primitive period lasted in undisputed sway we know not. All we know is, that at the dawn of authentic chronology we find that it has been long superseded by civilisation, – civilisation in the form of the ancient Oriental empires. These represent the then highest phase of evolution, the dominating power of the world as the curtain rises on the drama of history.

It is not difficult to see that the primitive social formation

16

is an instance of what Herbert Spencer would term "the instability of the homogeneous." All the oppositions and antagonisms expressed in civilisation are as yet latent; but although latent, they are none the less present and bound to manifest themselves in the end. The first stage of human society is based on the principle of kinship in its various gradations of proximity. This notion of kinship of itself implies an exclusiveness, an antagonism, which must sooner or later issue in civilisation, with its classes and races, and its class and race feuds. This, indeed, we may regard as the chief principle of change in prehistoric society, its chief solvent. It produced the earliest form of organisation, – organisation for military and predatory purposes. Hence the prominence of militaryism in all early civilisations; it having been out of the necessity of organisation for offensive and defensive objects that civilisation first arose.

The term prehistoric as applied to the first period of social man has a deeper meaning than as merely indicating that we have no written records concerning it; it may be taken to mean that the antagonisms, with the unravelling of which history is concerned, have not as yet manifested themselves. Nature was as yet identified with man, being regarded, that is to say, as a system of conscious beings like human society; the individual was identified with the race. Hence the echoes of the prehistoric period, – the period, that is, preceding civilisation, either in the history of the world as a whole, or of any special people present us with the dim and shadowy figures of gods and heroes moving across the stage, with scenes in which the processes of nature personified, stand for the deeds of human beings, and in which the movement or the custom of a whole people or tribe appear as the action of an individual man, – its legendary divine founder. This is what we call mythology. Prehistoric man, his customs, and beliefs, is the material of myth. Time has as yet no significance, Myth knows no chronology.

History, I take it, can hardly be better defined than as the unravelling of oppositions; the bringing to distinctness of latent contradictions, the realisation in their conflict, of mutually hostile tendencies. The oppositions wherein history – or, which is the same thing otherwise expressed, the development of the State, or of Civilisation, consists, may, I think, be reduced to two chief pairs, i.e., the opposition or antagonism between Nature and Mind, and the opposition, or antagonism between the Individual and the Society. The first opposition spoken of, that between external nature and the human mind, is more immediately of speculative, religious, and artistic significance; while the second, that between individual and society, of more immediately practical interest. But they are intimately connected with each other, and advance pari passu. In the antagonism between individual and society is contained the notion of personal ownership of property, with the whole state-machinery which is its expression. In the antagonism between nature and, mind is given religion, that is, religion in the sense of supernatural or spiritual religion, as opposed to the naive nature religions of early man. In the period of primitive communism and that which immediately succeeded it, religion, it must, always be remembered, had for its end and object the society; it was the idealistic expression of the life of the society. Man was concerned with nature, which he conceived as composed of beings like himself, only in so far as it affected the society, – the clan, the tribe, the people, etc. With the progress of civilisation and of the reflective consciousness accompanying it, man separated himself as a conscious being from nature, which became henceforward inert matter for him, governed by deities outside it. At a later period, wider generalisation subordinated these deities to one all-powerful conscious being, to whom they, as well as nature, were subordinated. It was with this being that man now concerned himself, rather than, as before, with the processes of nature per se. What interested him henceforward was the relation of himself

18

to this being. This became the subject-matter of religion, which ceased to occupy itself, as heretofore, with the life and movement of the community. Religion, now gradually ceasing to be social, became individual.

We have said that, what proximately led to the transformation of primitive communism into primitive civilisation was race or tribal exclusiveness, based on the notion of kinship, near or remote, through descent from some common divine ancestor, generally indicated by the possession of a common totem, – a plant or animal specially sacred to the clan or tribe. But within the historical period itself, we can distinguish progressive stages, which we shall see have been also determined by the same principle, – a principle by which the transformation of one form of civilisation into the other has been largely effected. The principle of political exclusiveness has contributed to break down every civilisation, thus paving the way for its successor. Let us now glance at that social whole of prehistoric times from which civilisation was a progressive departure, but yet which left such deep traces upon civilisation, especially in its earlier phases. Early society tends to expand from its simplest and closest form to others increasing in remoteness. The foundation of society, alike in the order of its nature and in the order of its history, is the blood-family. Now the earliest form of the blood-family may for practical purposes be identified with that which Lewis H. Morgan terms the Punalua family; where ascertainable, blood-relationship is recognised as precluding sexual intercourse, or, in other words, in which sexual relations are established on the basis of groups, from which children of the same mother of opposite sexes are excluded. [1] from this family-form the institution of the gens, or clan, directly proceeded; and the gens may be taken as the social basis of that earliest society properly so called, whose economic conditions are expressed in the phrase Primitive Communism: the foundation of the gens-formation primitive social organisation rested on. This formation,

19

all but universal as it is, presents infinite variety in points of detail in various peoples; but the main characteristics are the same. The second great division in the constitution of primitive society is the tribe. The tribe consists in a group of families, clans, or gentes, united together by some bond of consanguinity, either real or supposed. The tribe and gens are the component elements of the earliest organised society; they may seldom be found in isolation, but they are always distinguishable. Other and less important divisions there are [2], which vary according to time, place, and circumstances, but these need not detain us here. The dominating division primarily was doubtless the gens. At a later period the influence of the tribe; gained the upper hand.

But new economical conditions, the introduction of agriculture on a more extended scale, the taming of domestic animals, the acquirement of extensive property in flocks and herds and slaves (the captives taken in war), the beginnings of manufacture, perhaps more than all the improvement in weapons of war, necessitating a closer union and more systematic methods of offence and defence, led to a new social formation, destined to overshadow the original divisions of society. This was the consolidation, within a definite area, under definite institutions, of an aggregate of tribes – in most cases previously knit together in a loose manner as a "people" by supposed ties of remote kinship – into a social system called the city. By the word "city" as here used must not be understood the material city or place of habitation, but rather the society which originated it, and of which the material city, with its buildings, etc., was the outward expression. The city was the turning-point in human development; in it we pass from barbarism – primitive society – to civilisation. The organisation of tribes into a more or less coherent "people" denotes the highest phase of primitive barbaric society (see Appendix, III); the consolidation of the "people" into the organised "city" denotes the first stage in civilisation. (See Appendix, IV.) With the complete ascendency of the city, quâ city, over the earlier social forms within its pale, society has surrendered itself to the state. History – in the sense in which we use the word in the present article – has practically begun. But at the stage at which the city supersedes the gens and the tribe, a great change has already supervened in the primitive family organisation itself. The gens in its old form has fallen into abeyance, and the patriarchal family, with its despotic head, its wives, concubines, children, and slaves, which has sprung up out of it, now represents the unit of social life. Respecting the exact mode of the transformation of the gens-formation into the patriarchal family, we have but slight evidence; but it is nearly certain that from the first such authority or organising power as was necessary for the society was vested in the elders or fathers of the gens or tribe. This authority, as was natural, tended to grow and become regarded as sacred, together with the persons of its possessors. Hence the beginnings of despotism. [3]

The ancient form of the gens survives in the city, but it is mainly as a survival, and save for its being the central point of some of the most important religious sentiments and rites, tends to lose more and more of its significance; private property, though not necessarily individual property, has entered into the constitution of society. Classes arise in addition to the fundamental class division between slave and freeman, – classes within the free population of the city. But sometimes the city is not able to maintain an independent and separate existence. In this case it is in its turn absorbed into a larger unity, just as it had itself already absorbed the family and the tribe. This larger unity is the federation of cities (as it is in its origin), which subsequently becomes consolidated into the kingdom or empire, – such as Egypt, Assyria, Babylonia, Phoenicia, China, or India. The usual, although not invariable tendency is, for the imperial bond, at first loose and purely of the nature of a federal overlordship, to become drawn closer and closer until the city-state has in extreme cases become completely subordinated to the imperial state.

Such is the general description of the stages which, so far as we can see, led up to the vast Oriental civilisations with which universal history begins. In these, although more or less overshadowed and in abeyance, the earlier social forms are distinctly present as elements in the constitution of society. There is a family organisation, a tribal organisation, and a civic organisation, each with a special cultus of its own, and each presided over by its respective civil and religious head, on the principle of a hierarchy. The fact of the combination of sacerdotal and governmental functions in the same person shows us that religion is not as yet separated from the life of the community; that it still means no more than the ideal expression of social life a devotion to the social whole, and a care for all that contributes to its maintenance and well-being. Nature is as yet not formally separated from Man, not the individual from his social surroundings. The hearth and its sacred fire remains the central embodiment of the highest religious sentiment. The courts of the temples and the sacred fanes themselves are rendezvous for the business and pleasure of the citizens. But the antagonism is developing itself, and although not formally recognised, is every where present. A vast slave population has grown up in subordination to the tree, while the distinction between poor and rich grows ever more marked. With the leisure and culture which accumulation of wealth affords, the old naive belief in the unity of nature and man has become weakened and modified. With industrial development a new division frequently obtains, based not upon the old social principle of kinship, but upon the economical one of occupation. Certain families and tribes assume a particular order of handicraft or other employment which becomes hereditary, and to which they are fixed by custom or law. Thus a warrior caste, a sacerdotal caste, a manufacturing caste arises, the pre-eminent influence of the wealthy classes; composed of the more ancient families, culminating in the civil,

22

military, and religious chief. All we know of the ancient civilisations tends to show us that some such system as is here described prevailed in the earliest period of universal history, – in Egypt, Assyria, Babvlonia, the Palestine of Solomon's days, etc. But though the material antagonism between individual and community, no less than the speculative antagonism between nature and spirit, has begun, yet, judged from the standpoint of to-day, it may well seem but little developed in these civilisations. It is probable that extreme poverty and starvation were unknown in them as class-conditions; while, although private property-holding existed, the "absolute rights of property," in the modern sense of the word, were certainly unrecognised, since all property, in case of need, was at the disposal of the state. Religion, as we have already pointed out, concerned itself exclusively with the community, and with this world, and in no way with the individual and another world. The religions of antiquity, even when the earliest belief in the immediate personification of nature, was more or less on the wane, still conceived of man and nature as bound together by a system of subtle affinities, the knowledge of which was requisite to the well-being of the commonwealth, to the end that they might be regulated to its advantage. It was still the highest aspiration of the individual to found a family – that his life as part of the community should be immortal; as to his own personality, his only care was to devote himself to the city, and when his course was done, to go down to his fathers in the under-world of shades. Such science as existed consisted in astrology and magic, in accordance with the prevalent conception of the universe. It was a branch of the state-organisation, which kept in view the importance of the priestly caste, which in these early civilisations was the embodiment of the highest existing culture. (See Appendix, V.)

The Oriental monarchies began to be superseded about from the eighth to the sixth century BC by the Greek races. In the

Oriental monarchy the city tended to become strangled by the empire. When the free development of the city was once arrested, the whole civilisation began to stagnate or to crystallise into set forms. It then either lingered on for a time, like Egypt, or became the prey of free neighbouring peoples, like Assyria. Once the East became stationary, and the lead in human progress passed on to the peoples of Southeastern Europe; (first to the Greek communities and their colonies, and afterwards to those of Italy), where, owing to topographical and other causes, the city-form had not been superseded by the federal or imperial bond. It is, therefore, in these Aryan peoples of South-eastern Europe and in those of Asia Minor, that we meet with the purest type of the ancient city. All we have said hitherto respecting the city in its social and religious aspect applies with especial force to the classical city, more particularly in the earlier phases of its development. In this second period of ancient history the development of antagonism goes on apace, the mainspring of political development – the city – being henceforth free. In the cities of the classical world we have the most perfect specimens of the prehistoric tribal and gental forms, after they have been absorbed into the state. Nothing is plainer in classical history than the vitality of the old religious spirit. "The city," says Fustel de Coulanges, speaking of the classical city, "was founded on religion and constituted like a church. Hence its power; hence also its omnipotence and the absolute empire it exercised over its members. In a society established on such principles individual liberty could not exist. The citizen was subject in all things and without reserve to the city; he belonged to it entirely. The religion which had given birth to the city, and the city which regulated religion, were not two things, but one. These two powers, associated and inseparable, constituted an almost superhuman might, to which mind and body were alike subject." For a long time after the antagonism of interest between individual and community was strongly developed in the economic sphere, the great end of religion and morality still continued to be social. The introspective ethics of individualism were not from the first so

24

congenial to the Aryan races as they were to the Semitic.

In the cities of the classical world we have a wealth of material preserved, in which we may trace individual interest steadily gaining the upper hand over social interest; while at the same time the supernatural view of the universe and man's relation to it as steadily supersedes the old naive and natural one. Here also, as in the Oriental world, a slave-holding production, of which direct exploitation of human labour-power was the special foam, tended to supersede all free labour. This was now exercised for the benefit of the individual rich citizen, and not, as in earlier stages, for that of the gens, the tribe, or the city. The religion, again, notwithstanding the vigorous survival of its original forms, steadily gave way before the advance of individualism; it inevitably became less social and more personal. The various "mysteries" which sprang into vogue, many of them imported from the East, had for their end the setting forth of the mystical relation of the individual to the supposed divinity outside nature. The gods themselves gradually became transported to a heaven above the nature and society of which previously they were simply the personifications. The ghosts of ancestors, too, became relegated to the same super-sensible sphere. But these tendencies cannot be said to have fully realised themselves until the city-form had been reduced to a meaningless phrase, had developed its own contradiction, in the great city-empire of Rome; although from the earliest period in which the Greek cities appear on the arena of history we can see them at work. As already stated, at first the classical city seems to embody considerable traces of the primitive communistic society out of which it arose; but as the Greek cities developed, productive labour came to be more and more relegated to the slave population, who far exceeded the limited number of freemen. Exchange of commodities – commerce – now took place on a much more extended scale than before, – a circumstance facilitated by the opening of the Egyptian ports. The internal struggle which characterised the

25

growth of the Greek or Roman states between the rich minority and poor majority of free inhabitants of the city was the framework within which the principle of individualism in economics asserted itself in the ancient world. (See Appendix, VI.) It is important to understand the meaning of these struggles, which in their main features seem so uniform in character. Their meaning would seem to be this. The so-called democracies of the classical cities were really a middle class, in many cases composed largely of aliens, or at least persons belonging to none of the older gentes. In breaking down the ancient aristocracies they were really breaking down the social institutions which had descended from early society, but which in the course of time had lost meaning, or redounded merely to the advantage of a clique of privileged families. The strife between the aristocratic and democratic factions was a struggle for political equality among the free men. But on neither side was there any idea, of the great slave majority of the state having any rights at all. The economic development made the individual citizen's gain and advancement, whether as trader, mercenary soldier, or professional politician, a point of first importance in life. But even in spite of this the religious bond of solidarity with the city-state sufficed to prevent the complete ascendancy of individual over social interest (in the limited sense in which the latter was then understood). The state had not as yet entirely lost its social character; it had not quite degenerated into a mere machine for protecting property and privilege. Now just as the material ascendancy of individual interest was undermining the old religious sentiment described, there; appeared on the market-place at Athens a teacher, giving utterance to a doctrine which implied the undermining of it from its moral side. In the "Know thyself" of Socrates we have the first expression in the Greek world of that personal morality as opposed to the old social morality, which culminated in the Christianity of later ages. The Athenians felt instinctively the danger of this new ethic, and in a panic condemned Socrates to death for proclaiming it. (See Appendix, VII) But it had taken root already, and the writings of Plato and Aristotle exhibit the

26

two moralities in conflict and an ineffectual attempt to reconcile them. From this time forward the progressive weaning of the mind from its old conception of nature, and its old satisfaction in the "city," becomes marked; although it was given to the dreamy Semitic rather than to the practical Aryan intellect to be the typical exponent of the new tendency. The races of South-eastern Europe were destined in the ancient world to work out the opposition of interest between individual and society on its economical side; but for a satisfactory ethic of Individualism they had to look to Western Asia. This ethnical peculiarity is illustrated by the unsatisfactoriness of the Greek attempts in this direction, which, although making much noise with the educated, evoked but little enthusiasm even among their votaries, and none among ordinary men. We refer, of course, to the various philosophical sects – Cynic, Cyreniac, Stoic, Epicurean – which arose during the declining period of Greek independence. As the old political life of the Greek cities was dying out, the cultivated citizen turned his attention to the question of the most satisfactory manner in which he, as an individual, could spend his life. The "philosopher" and the "virtuous man," wrapped up in himself, superseded the "citizen" among the educated classes. The thoughtful man began to feel disgust at the old morality which was limited in its application to the single city-state, and did not apply to all the members of that. Yet he in vain searched for something satisfactory to supply its place.

Such was the Greek world when the victorious Roman armies destroyed the last vestige of Greek independence by reducing the country to a Roman province, from which event the "lead" in historical progress – i.e., in the development of the dual opposition between individual and society, and between nature and spirit – passed on to the new city-empire. In imperial Rome, as already observed, the ancient city-form evolved its own contradiction. The moment the city became an imperial centre, owning nominal citizens among every people, its citizenship being reduced to a mere commercial value, from that time forward it is plain that the sacredness, the meaning, the reality of the ancient city-form had passed away. The last vestige of primitive society with the political exclusiveness it implied had given place to a cosmopolitanism in which social solidarity lingered solely as a survival in the official religion, and in which in reality individual interest alone obtained. Historically the function of the Roman empire answers in the political sphere to the function of Christianity in the religious sphere, namely, the destruction of the tribal and race exclusiveness, which had had its day. (See Appendix, VIII.) This meant on its obverse side absolute predominance of the individual – i.e., of individual interest – in the one case in economics, in the other in ethics and religion.

The earlier historical development of the Roman city does not differ essentially from that of the Greek cities; but our information is fuller in the one case than in the other. We can trace the development of oppositions more in detail in Roman history. Rome is the type of the later classical evolution. As soon as all public offices were thrown open to the Plebeian, all public life became a scramble for wealth. The antagonism between private and common interest, or, which is the same thing, between individual and community, manifested itself here, as elsewhere, in the degeneration of the gentes which had originally formed the whole city into a privileged aristocratic class within the city. This naturally brought in its train the opposition of all elements of later date. The struggle of these elements for equality meant the breaking down of the now obsolete survivals of the ancient communal and tribal system, and its complete reconstruction on the basis of wealth and individual property. For these opposing classes (the Plebs) it must be remembered had little or no tribal solidarity among themselves. They were composed largely of heterogeneous elements, the only bond of cohesion between them being the city within whose domains they dwelt, and for which they fought, but from the inner civil and religious system of which they were for a long time excluded, and which in consequence it was their aim to deprive as far as possible of its meaning. The Plebs, at first, largely consisted of small farmers and poor handicraftsmen who worked for their living; but with the development of the State politically and economically, with the great slave imports derived from foreign conquest, etc., a wealthy commercial Plebs arose, and it was this Plebs that profited by the reforms in the constitution, while in the same proportion the poorer Plebs became less and less able to cope with the slave-holding production now becoming universal. This poorer class of freemen must, indeed, have succumbed altogether, or else have created a social revolution, had it not been for the fact that to the last so much primitive communism remained in the Roman state-system that no free citizen could starve, since he could always obtain sufficient for his maintenance from public resources. With the conquest of Greece, BC 146, Rome inherited the more advanced culture of the Greek world. By this means progress in civilisation – or, which is the same thing, progress in corruption – was enormously accelerated. The Gracchan legislation marks the period of the complete ascendency of Roman Bourgeoisdom as such. From this time forward the power of the money-bag was supreme. The imperial policy itself no longer had for its object the glory of the city, but simply and solely the conquest of new provinces for the sake of the aggrandisement either by direct plunder or by oppressive taxation, of the particular party which happened to be in power in Rome, together with its enormous army of dependents.

In morality and religion the same symptoms we have already noticed as belonging to the decline of Greek independence appear in an intensified form – i.e., the withdrawal of culture and intelligence from public affairs, and their concentration on the individual and the problem of his happiness. All the Greek sects, claiming to offer a solution of this now all-important problem, spread rapidly. These, to a large extent, sought the conditions of happiness in this life. But there was another and deeper phase of the same movement which was characterised by a contempt for nature, society, and this world, and a concentration on the notion of another life beyond the grave. This craving was sought to be satisfied by the introduction of new mystical Oriental cults, and in various other ways. To be brief, these symptoms of the divorce of the individual from the life of the state, and his concentration on himself, together with those of the rise of a speculative dualism between nature and spirit, alike found their ultimate idealistic expression in the great Semitic creed – Christianity, – the religion of individual salvation and of the other world. The accentuation of the practical antagonism between individual and community, between private and public interest, and of the speculative antagonism between nature and spirit, between this world and the other world, went on apace as the twilight of ancient civilisation gradually deepened into darkness.

The outward shell of the forms of ancient city life, rotten through and through, was shattered in the fifth and sixth centuries by the German tribes, fresh from their primitive village communities. In the establishment of Christianity, personal as opposed to social morality and the religion of another world, as opposed to the ancient social religions of this world, had first, received official expression. The Christian empire accordingly presented both economically and ethically a more complete triumph of the principle of individualism over the principle of socialism than the world had seen before. The opposition between the various phases of human life was becoming concentrated in the great antithesis of the Middle Ages between religious and secular. The Graeco-Roman world steadily progressed from its earlier communistic form, in which the city was all in all towards the ascendency of individual interest here and hereafter; and the progress culminated in its death as a civilisation. But the economic forms of which civilisation is capable had as yet not all been passed through. The classical development was limited in various ways; first it was limited ethnically, it centred itself in one particular branch of the Aryan race, the Graeco-Roman, and left entirely out of account another equally important branch, the Teutonic; secondly, it was limited economically by the conditions of a slave-holding production. This is essentially different from our modern capitalistic production. Men had as yet imperfectly learnt the art of buying in order to sell again; the middleman was absent. The wealthy Roman purchased what slave handicraftsmen and labourers he could, and enriched himself directly by their labour. The element of exchange value per se, which rules to-day with a rod of iron, entered in a very minor degree into the constitution of classical society. Trade would seem to have been viewed by the classic much as card-sharping is by us. Thus Cicero, in his De Officiis, speaks of trade as disreputable, while Suetonius says of the Emperor Vespasian: "He likewise engaged in a pursuit disgraceful even in a private individual; buying great quantities of goods, for the purpose of selling them again to advantage." It is obvious, therefore, that the great economic expression of an individualistic society- viz., commerce – had very imperfectly established itself in the classical world. It was not until humanity had passed through another distinct period of development, a period in which the Teutonic races were the chief actors, – that the opposition between individual and society attained the completeness towards which it tended.

The German tribes of the time of the Roman Empire, already constituted as "peoples," being in the highest phase of barbarism, and on the verge of civilisation, were (since the germ of a new society was already present in them) the fittest instruments for the transformation of the effete civilisation of antiquity into a new world. The German, fresh from his nature worship and his tribal communities, was precipitated headlong

31

into a civilisation with its antagonisms fully developed – that is, as fully developed as was compatible with the then current economic conditions. The great industry being non-existent, the then world market having collapsed from various obvious causes, the old slave production became unprofitable. Vast numbers of slaves were, therefore, virtuously and religiously manumitted, in order to save the expense of their maintenance.

"Slavery," says Engels, "ceased to pay, and, therefore, it died out. But it left its sting behind it in the freeman's contempt for productive labour ... Slavery was economically impossible, the labour of freemen was morally despised. The one had ceased to be, the other had not begun to be the ground-form of social production. The only help here was a complete revolution."

And, in fact, an economic as well as a racial revolution did take place. The feudal system, which was the ultimate issue or this revolution, was nothing else than primitive communistic society, with the notion of sovereignty on the part of the head of the community super-added. It is true, this was a modification of the first importance, but it must not be forgotten that it was limited in many ways, and that it did not prevent the serf of the Middle Ages from being, as a rule, in a far better condition than the slave of antiquity, not to speak of the modern labourer.

Religion had in the medieval period a twofold aspect. On the one side was the Church hierarchy, the legacy of the Roman Empire, on the model of whose organisation it was formed. This, with its elaborate body of semi-pagan ceremonials, customs, and rites, entered closely into the whole political and social constitution of the Middle Ages. As a political power it claimed supreme jurisdiction over emperors and kings. Its superior clergy and religious corporations were themselves powerful feudal

32

potentates, possessing vast territories with all the rights of independent sovereigns. As a social power its influence, its rites, ceremonies and superstitions, entered into all relations in life. It gave a religious colouring to every department of human interests. Even the merchant guilds, and after them the craft guilds, were in a sense religious bodies, – a fact which served Henry VIII with a plausible excuse; for confiscating their property under the edict abolishing the religious orders. Side by side with this aspect of religion in which it simply ideally expressed the general social and political life of the community much in the same way as the religions of antiquity, was its essentially Christian aspect, that of a personal, introspective, and spiritualistic theory of the universe and of life. This more distinctively Christian side of Catholicism, although never dominant daring the Middle Ages, was continually manifesting itself in a sporadic manner; its most remarkable products being Francis of Assisi and Thomas à Kempis. It influenced in some cases those who sought refuge from the world in the monasteries and various religious brotherhoods that arose, having personal holiness anal salvation as their aim. But it never entered into the ordinary everyday life of the average man and woman, as was subsequently the case with Protestantism. The barbarians had accepted Christianity; they accepted, that is, a religion which in its inner significance belonged to a period of ultra-civilisation, which was the supreme expression of the revolt of the individual against the old social morality and against the old conception of the universe; in short, which pre-supposed a long development. Much of the old tribal morality of the Germans, and many of their old modes of thought continued, therefore, to exist under the sanction of the Church, and to this we owe the chivalry and "honour" of the Middle Ages, besides mach of their folk-lore and superstition. Add to this that the Church itself, modelled as it was externally on the Roman imperial system had absorbed, with but little modification, large fragments of classical paganism, But, as we have said; the individualism and super-naturalism of Christianity subsisted side by side with the semi-paganism of the

33

popular creed. It was always the ultimate court of appeal, and supplied what was considered as the highest object in life – namely, preparation for another world. The poetry, the chivalry, the enthusiasm of the Middle Ages are clearly traceable to their barbaric side, and in no wise to the creed of the blasé Roman world. (See Appendix, IX.) The Medieval mind had reserved to itself the idea of two separate spheres, a religious and a secular. To the "secular" man religion consisted in external and pagan observances, in consideration of which the Church guaranteed his ultimate salvation. It was only to the monastic recluse, and rarely even to him, that religion was a personal matter. Not until the final disruption of the mediaeval system and the ascendancy of the middle class Protestant creed, did the theory of individual freedom of contract here and hereafter come into general vogue. The Church, in spreading its glamour over every department of human life, from war to handicraftship, which thus came to have a mystical religious significance attaching to them, was only fulfilling the function and acting as the succedaneum of the old family, tribal, and social religion of the heathen German; in which the opposition between sacred and profane did not exist. The medieval instinct with true logicality felt that it was needful for the man who aspired to the truly and specially Christian ideal of personal holiness to come out of a world in which the personality merely counted as part of the general social hierarchy.

We may divide the Middle Ages into two epochs. The first, the period of Feudalism proper, that is, of production on a small scale for use on the feudal estate, in which exchange was very limited. This period we may roughly assign to from the eighth to the thirteenth century. Towards its close a surplus began to be produced for purposes of commerce. Markets for the exchange of necessaries and luxuries became more numerous. Finally, independent townships arose, that is, the villains clustered together on the larger estates, especially the ecclesiastical, shook off the more onerous feudal dues in consideration of an annual rental, while within these towns a distinct industrial system arose under the auspices of the guilds. This brings us to the second period of the Middle Ages, which may also be approximately assigned to from the thirteenth to the sixteenth century. This is the flourishing age of the guild industry, and during this period arose the first form of the opposition between middle class and proletariat. The guilds naturally soon developed into close corporations, entry to which became hedged round with ever-increasing expenses and difficulties. For all that the great social struggle of the period was between the burghers and the nobles. The typical instance of this straggle is the revolt in the Netherlands under the Arteveldtes against the Count of Flanders. The gradually lapsing power of feudalism proper was shown in the comparative freedom the agricultural serf had acquired, and the attempt to deprive him of which in England was the main cause of the Wat Tyler insurrection. This interesting and important period to be properly dealt with demands a separate treatise.

In the sixteenth century the antagonism latent in mediaeval society had reached, a point of development which was incompatible with the continued existence of that society. The world-market was opening up. The middle classes had become one of the most important factors in civilisation. The modern national systems of Europe were becoming fixed. Trade and industry were everywhere in the ascendant. Beside,, this, the Christian religion was emerging from the semi-pagan form it had assumed during the Middle Ages, and asserting in their fulness the individualist and introspective tendencies peculiar to it. The distinction between religious and secular was only broken down on one side to reappear with increased asperity on another. Protestantism proclaimed the doctrine of personal salvation by faith alone – i.e., the whole of religion was resolved into a purely personal matter, with reference to which, as extreme Protestant sects like the Puritans very logically maintained, a Church tradition and organisation were entirely superfluous. In Protestantism the supremacy of individualism in religion, its antagonism to the old social religions, reaches its highest point of development. It has shaken off the last fragment of pagan poetry and sentiment, if not of pagan doctrine. It is personal and matter of fact. Under Protestantism religion has become necessarily divorced from worldly avocations. The continual interruption to industry, the time allowed by Catholicism in its festivals and holidays for enjoyment, not less than the time exacted for penance, etc., could not be tolerated. The rising middle classes were beginning to find out the "dignity of labour," that it was appointed to men to work, etc., and that the longer the journeyman worked, and the less time he wasted in amusement, the better it was for his soul and their bodies.

History from the sixteenth century downwards is a picture of the struggle of the rising middle or manufacturing and trading classes, to emancipate themselves from the trammels of the feudal or landowning classes, and thereby to attain to individual freedom of action in the furthering of private interests. Of the causes, such as the dissolution of the old feudal estates, the appropriation of common lands, the new inventions, etc., which all contributed to bring about the rise of capitalism as the leading economical form of society, it is unnecessary to say anything in this place; our purpose here being, to suggest the ultimate meaning of universal history from the point of view of modern socialism, rather than to expound the modus operandi of historic evolution. There is one fact, however, to be noted which is extremely significant, namely, that the ascendancy of the middle classes in the shape they now assumed was incompatible with the continued existence of the old guild organisations. The guilds had the reason of their being in feudal privilege and landed tenure like the nobles; like the latter the power of these great municipal monopolies began rapidly and hopelessly to decline in proportion to the strides mane by the new individualist capitalism. The

36

middle class of the second medieval period (as we have termed it) was essentially an aristocracy. The medieval city of the fifteenth century was in some respects a kind of rude reflex of the classical city; If we like to carry out the parallel, we may compare the guildsmen to the patricians, the journeymen to the plebeians, and the apprentices, who were in statu pupillari, and, therefore, without rights at all, to the slave class. The new capitalistic middle class differed from the guildsmen of old as the new proletariat, the precursor of the proletariat of to-day, differed from the merry journeymen of the mediaeval township.

But the meaning of history since the close of the medieval period is so plain as to be unmistakable. Every political aspiration, every political reform, has meant a breaking asunder of the bonds which held the old civilisation together, the freeing of the individual from the duties now obsolete which bound him in some sort to the social whole. In Economics the middle-class revolution accomplished itself immediately through the subdivision of labour and the workshop system, the so-called periode manufacturère, in the course of which the master gradually ceased to be himself a worker, and became an overseer. The gradual and apparently limitless unfolding of the world-market assisted the development, but its final phase was reached in the great machine industry which from the last quarter of the eighteenth century to our own day bas been steadily progressing.

In Politics the movement was characterised by the consolidation of the European nationalities (in the Middle Ages loose feudal confederacies), which was accomplished by (1) bureaucratic centralisation; (2) the extension of royal prerogative; and (3) the rise of modern commercial patriotism. Its great political expression is Constitutionalism – i.e., the real supremacy of the middle classes in the State, though this may in some cases be varnished over by the nominal ascendancy of the older order,

37

as in England. This was finally and definitely attained by the French Revolution of 1789.

In Religion it is expressed in the accentuation of the Protestant doctrine before alluded to, of "the religion of the heart," that is, of the working out of your own salvation, as opposed to the mediaeval Catholic doctrine, that belonging to the Church organisation itself constitutes a claim to the Kingdom of Heaven. This is a theme upon which the evangelical preacher is never tired of enlarging. It is also shown in the separation of religion from daily life, as expressed in the emphasis laid upon the distinction between sacred and profane; in short, in the modern Protestant notion of reverence. (See Appendix, X.) To the medieval mind, trinity, saints, and angels were little more than a company of boon companions, whose adventures could be represented on the stage of any village fair with edification to the beholder. The miracle-plays extant (which it must be remembered were played often by priests themselves, and always under the auspices of the Church) contain what the modern Protestant mind would deem blasphemies, compared to which those of Mr. George Foote are reverential. The notion of "reverence," like that of personal religion, is the creation of that middle-class order which took its first rise in the sixteenth, and has culminated in the world of the nineteenth century.

In its Morality the individualistic character of the movement is no less apparent than in its religion. Bourgeois morality is eminently personal. A man in his public acts, in all he does that concerns the people, may prove himself an ill-conditioned ruffian or an unscrupulous adventurer, careless though he plunge a whole nation into misery to serve his own purposes or ambition; he may be a Napoleon III, a Prince Imperial, a Bartle Frere, a Gordon; yet he may still, if he only make himself sufficiently prominent, expect honourable mention

38

when living and a public monument when dead. All is fair it is said in love and war. This principle is nowadays commonly extended to public life, and in politics all is fair that tends to personal advancement. The man who takes a serious view of social and political duty is an enthusiast or a fool to be laughed at. Not so he who can persuade the public, whether truly or not, that he is that rather washed-out product of the nineteenth century, the "man without a vice." This man extolled for the "purity" of his life may commit any public rascality he pleases; on the other hand, if an offence against the conventional personal ethics were brought home to a man, it would be deemed sufficient to blast the most single-minded public career.

And what does this middle-class order mean with its isolation of every aspect or department of human life from every other? The only answer that can be given on the lines of the foregoing argument is that it denotes the final phase of Civilisation. Here the antitheses, latent in primitive human society, for the first time reach their fullest development. The cardinal practical antagonism (as we have termed it) between individual and community has resulted in the complete subjection of social or public, to individual or private interest. Ever since civilisation began, the aim of man has been to free himself as individual from what he conceived to be his bondage to the social whole. The moment he distinguished his private interest or property from the public interest or property of the society of which he was hart, from that moment did history begin in its long array of crimes, tyrannies, and slaughters. An economic and social individualism necessarily implied sooner or later a change in the conception of duty. With the abstraction of individual interest from its relation to the common interest of society came that other abstraction expressed in the great speculative antagonism between Nature and Spirit, World and God, Body and Soul, etc. This speculative antagonism has reacted on the practical; it has superseded the old ethical sentiment by placing

39

the individual man's highest object of duty and devotion, not in the society without him, but in the Divinity believed to be revealed within him; by placing the goal of human aspiration, not in this world, but in another world; by lulling individuals and classes into condoning their sufferings here by holding out imaginary hopes of bliss hereafter. Thus has the natural been completely subjugated by the spiritual in the popular theology and ethics.

The principles here indicated were nearly, although not quite (for reasons before stated), realised in the decadent period of the Roman Empire. Now, at last, they are present in their rankest growth, and constitute the essence of our nineteenth-century world. Along a steep and tortuous path man has attained to a complete civilisation. Above the gods, said the Greeks, are the fates; and a strange fate it is which has lured, nay, forced, man forward by the very necessities of his existence, under the pretence of realising his liberty as an individual, to such a shrine as this. Now, in a sense, the goal of the march of history is attained, attained in the victory of principles which are the antithesis of those under the auspices of which civilisation started, but whose ultimate victory civilisation implied. In the well-known phrase, "Every man for himself, and God for us all," or in that other phrase, which is, indeed, the same thing otherwise expressed, "The devil take the hindmost," we have a rough and concise statement of that principle of individualism and of the relegation of religion to a supersensible sphere, which together form the pillars of the modern world.

But have these principles, for which so many in days gone by have fought and bled, have they realised the happiness expected of them? Here they are; you have it now all for which you have craved. And what has it proved? Now that the fruit of individualism is plucked; by the virtual admission of every

40

thinking person, whether socialist or not, it is but Dead Sea fruit after all. In the supremacy of individual interest here and hereafter was seen the mirage of human happiness and progress. Once attained, and behold the fancied happiness is an illusion; hence that characteristic product of the present day – cynical pessimism. The ordinary mind sees the illusion, but cannot see beyond it – cannot see that the mirage which has lured men on, although in itself a phantasm, is yet the foretaste of a reality more distant, yet none the less real for that; and that the dreary waste which the place of the mirage proved to be, had to be traversed before the reality lying below its horizon could be reached.

In the present day the abstract, the nominal freedom of the individual is complete. But individualism has no sooner shaken itself free from the supports which, though they may have cumbered it in its advance, yet did at least keep it from falling; it has no sooner completely realised itself, than its death-knell is rung, and it finds itself strangled by the very economical revolution which had rendered its existence possible. For that revolution which has brought about an absolute separation of classes, has deprived the one class of all individuality whatever, albeit their abstract freedom still remains to mock them. Production in its process has become more than ever before social and co-operative, notwithstanding that its end and object is more than ever before mere individual aggrandisement. The majority are the slaves of modern Industrialism. Individualism, therefore, for the majority has become a meaningless phrase. The same with supernatural religion. The distinction between God and World has practically ceased to exist for the educated classes. With the Hegelian philosophy and that vast body of contemporary thought which, whether consciously or unconsciously, is the outcome of that philosophy, the distinction survives merely as a conventional phrase.

What, then, does all this point to, if it does not point to the fact that civilisation, having accomplished its end in social evolution, must cease to be; that it must suffer a transformation, in the course of which its essential nature will be abolished? Its essential nature, as we have sought to show, consists in antagonism – antagonism of class, creed, nationality. It involves an isolation or abstraction of every aspect of human life from every other; it is the direct negation of the communistic solidarity in which the nature of prehistoric society consisted, and in which politics, morality, religion, and art were as yet undivided from each other, and from the life of the whole. Now, civilisation, we have said, is the negation of this primitive society as implying universal division, strife, and opposition. But if the next stage in evolution implies the negation of the opposition of which civilisation consists, it must mean a return in a sense to the conditions of primitive society. Two negations make an affirmation. The negation of civilisation, which is itself the negation of early society, must therefore, mean a return to the essential characteristic of that society – i.e., Solidarity, Communism, or Socialism. We say the essential characteristic, as, of course, although the socialised world of the future will present a correspondence with the socialised world of the past, it, will be a correspondence on a higher plane – a likeness in difference. The passage from Primitive Communism to the Communism of the future was only possible through the mediation of History otherwise expressed, of Individualism. It was impossible for the race solidarity, on which early society was based, and which is implied in its economies, in its ethics, in its religion, and its art, to pass at once into that human solidarity for which we are preparing to-day. The race barrier had to be broken down, effectually and completely, and this could only be done by the temporary sacrifice of the social principle itself. The early solidarity of kinship had to be resolved into its direct antithesis – individualism, universal and world-wide. Individualism in economics, in ethics, in religion, was the necessary intermediate step before the final goal of universal solidarity or communism, which unites the solidarity of early society with the cosmopolitan principle of individualism, could be reached. The society of the future will not be limited by consideration of kinship or of frontier, as was the society of the past. It will embrace the whole world, irrespective of race, in so far as it has overcome civilisation and become socialised. The test will be one of principle, not of blood. The infirmities of early society, its spirit of race exclusiveness, with its unconsciousness of the meaning of the changes it underwent, its ignorance of nature, its crudity of conception, – these things have passed away for ever. Yet none the less will the society of the future, to which socialists look forward, be a society in which all interests are again united, since they will all have a definite social aim; in other words, since the interest of the individual will be once more identified, and this time consciously, with the interest of the community; and lastly, since our ideal will cease to have for its object God and "another world," and be brought back to its original sphere of social life and "this world."

How or when this great revolution will take place we are not now concerned to discuss; whether, as some think, the Slav races of the East will be the chief actors in it, or whether it will be carried out by the older Western nations. To the present writer there seems a kind of solemnity in the drama of universal history – of humanity overcome and crucified by the wealth and organisation which is the work of its own hand. It is only relieved by the thought that the old Pagan-Christian myth of purification through suffering is susceptible of a new application here. Mankind having passed through the fire of the state-world, of Civilisation, of history, must come out the stronger and more perfect. Latterday society redeemed from Civilisation will be a higher and a more enduring society than that early society which knew no Civilisation. It is towards this world, where Civilisation shall have ceased to be, that the socialist of to-day casts his eyes. In this he has a right to feel that in a literal sense his faith and his

43

hope is founded on the "rock of ages;" that where the ages are for him, nought can be against him.

"There amidst the world new budded shall our earthly deeds abide,

Though our names be all forgotten, and the tale of how we died."

Notes

1. For a full description of this primitive form of the family, see Morgan's Ancient Society, also Engels' Ursprung der Familie.

2. E.g., the so-called Phraterie.

3. It is in the Semitic peoples that the patriarchal phase in the evolution of the family is most strongly marked, and shows the greatest tenacity of life. In the Aryan races it is it general much less accentuated, and consequently tends to pass away much sooner. The Romans, however, form a noteworthy exception in this respect.

# A French Economist on Collectivism[1]
# (July 1884)

Some one (Macaulay I think) said that a new doctrine passed through three stages, that of ridicule, argument, and acceptance. The new Economy, must have certainly reached the second of these stages, to judge by the flood of literature, which pretends to be serious in combating the theory of Scientific Socialism, that is pouring from the press both English and foreign. Whether the traditional Economists will reach the third stage, ere the shadow of death overtakes them and the society they represent, is doubtful. There is one virtue conspicuously absent in English writers on the same side, which strikes one at the first glance in M. Leroy-Beaulieu's new work. He has certainly read what he is professing to criticise, but beyond this our praise for his fairness can hardly extend. His book is from beginning to end a tissue of cases of verbal quibble, of ignoratio elenchi, and here and there even, we fear, of wilful misrepresentation. We do not know whether it is the moral or the intellectual side of M. Leroy-Beaulieu's character that is to blame for these things, but there they are.

In an introductory chapter the author sketches the progress of Socialism within the last few years. He here endeavours to fix the terms Socialist, Collectivist, Communist. The first he justly regards as generic, covering a variety of views more or less divergent. But the retention of the term Communism for the crude utopic conception of the direct, equal and periodical division of the objects of consumption, involves an ignoring of the more recent history of the word, which is surely, to say the least, injudicious. However, if we once grant M. Leroy-Beaulieu his definitions, we must admit that he adheres to them fairly

45

consistently throughout. A general and somewhat discursive criticism follows (embracing Henry George, Laveleye, Marx, Schäffle, &c.), of the charges brought by Socialist and semi-Socialist writers against the current economic régime. This includes some chapters on primitive Communism, types of which are found in the Russian Mir and the Javan village community. The first division of the book terminates with a somewhat rambling homily on the terrible results likely to ensue from land-nationalisation. The second part is devoted to a more systematic attempt at criticism of the theoretic portions of Marx and Schäffle. (By-the-bye, why does M. Leroy-Beaulieu exclude the writings of Frederic Engels and Rodbertus from his animadversions?).

In an ordinary magazine review it is obviously impossible to touch upon all the points raised in a work such as the present. We are, therefore, forced to confine ourselves to a few typical instances of M. Leroy-Beaulieu's mode of treatment. An attempt is made at starting to confound sundry definitions established among Socialists. The method, we may observe, of obliterating real distinctions by verbal jugglery, and thus apparently landing an opponent in a reductio-ad-absurdum, is a specious one, and a favourite with sophists. By taking a conception in its most abstract sense, carefully emptying it of all empirical content, it is easy enough to make everything nothing and nothing everything. It is this which Hegel means when he declares the identity of Being and non-Being. The pure abstract form of any conception can be turned inside out or outside in without making any difference. Thus the wily Liberal posed the honest Home-Ruler, who was pleading for his cause on the ground of the right of peoples to self-government, by contending that if Ireland were justified in detaching itself from the United Kingdom, so, on like grounds, was any English county, town, or even any group of persons inhabiting a particular plot of land, and that ergo the right of Ireland to self-government was illusory. Now M. Leroy-

Beaulieu, as we were saying, tries this dialectical trick on. But he is not altogether successful in the performance. A little more practice is wanted. For instance, in seeking (p.17) to prove the fallacy of the distinction between Bourgeois and Proletaire, he asks whether the well-salaried manager of a wealthy company, or the captain of a large vessel, &c., inasmuch as these cannot be said to possess the instruments with which they work, are therefore to be ranked as proletaires; adding that if so, nine-tenths of those the Socialists disdainfully term Bourgeois are Proletaires. The answer to this is obvious, viz., that these middle-men are placed in a position of advantage with reference to the instruments of production which practically amounts pro tanto to possession. This position of advantage may arise from social connections, exceptional ability, or other things, but anyway it lifts them out of the arena of the labour market, and gives them a control (more or less) over the means of production, which the proletaire has not. Again, M. Leroy-Beaulieu sneeringly complains that, under a Collectivist régime, no one would be allowed to mend his neighbour's trousers or shirt for a monetary consideration, inasmuch as he would be then employing his needle and thread for purposes of production, which would be a return to Individualism, and hence illegal. Let M. Leroy-Beaulieu reassure himself. All those who desire, to make a living by an individualistic mending of shirts and trousers will be allowed full liberty to satisfy their aspirations. We will not vouch for their being much patronised, for the probability of repairs of this character being executed better, more rapidly, and with less expenditure of labour in the State or communal factory is great. But, any way they would have their economic liberty to fatten on.

We find the assumption running through the whole of M. Leroy-Beaulieu's book that the collectivist intends to suppress private production and exchange by prohibitory laws. This is a crucial instance of his want of grasp of the subject. Is it by prohibitory laws that the grande industrie has supplanted the petite industrie in well-nigh every branch of production? Prohibitory laws will be quite unnecessary when private enterprise ceases to be profitable, as it must when the whole of the means of production, distribution, and credit, on a large scale, are in the possession of the people themselves. References to primitive communism, whether as established in the Russian Mir, the Javan village, or the ancient German commune, are obviously quite pointless as arguments in discussing the organisation of the future, for the simple reason that they belong to an anterior moment of social evolution. Primitive undifferentiated Communism develops its own contradiction; a progress to some form of Individualism is inevitable; this again in its turn discovers within itself the germs of destruction. In the very act of realising its fullest and most complete life, its doom is sealed. The individual ceases to be producer, although possessing full control over the exchange of the commodities produced. The next step in progress is the differentiated Communism or Collectivism, which with the production already more than half-way socialised, completes the process, and gives to the community a control over the exchange of that which is its collective product.[2]

To confute the Collectivist by proving what he never doubts, namely, the tendency of primitive Communism to issue in Individualism is surely an ignoratio elenchi of the baldest kind. Yet an important portion of M. Leroy-Beaulieu's criticism is based thereon. "Faut il recommencer," says M. Leroy-Beaulieu, p.150, "une experience deja faites pendant de longs siècles et qui a echoué partout." The fact is, of course, that the experience has never been made and never could have been made till now. Our author evidently regards progress as linear. A very little acquaintance with the course of historic development would have sufficed to show him that (if we may employ metaphor in the matter) it is rather spiral, that is, that the same fact invariably returns in a higher form, in short that the straight line theory is a fallacy. Even Mr. Herbert Spencer recognises this in a manner.

48

And if it be recognised, what becomes of the argument that because one form of collective ownership was the economic beginning of Social evolution, that therefore another form cannot be regarded as the end. (See pp.148, et seq.)

We must confess to being surprised at the apparent inability of a Professor of Political Economy at the College de France to grasp the distinction between mere production per se and capitalistic production. We are told that Robinson in his island would have had capital if he had given himself the trouble to construct a wheelbarrow, since everything is capital that tends to increase the productivity of human labour. This again is either crass ignorance or a mere quibble about words, and does not really upset existent distinctions. It is quite clear that a radical distinction exists between production for the sake of using the product, and production for the sake of effecting a gain on the exchange of the product. It is this latter kind of production that Marx understands in accordance with current usage, as capitalistic production. To say that our ancestors of the stone age possessed capital in so far as they had flint implements wherewith to fashion their spear-heads, and that the distinction between these and the locomotive is only one of degree is certainly to evade the question. M. Leroy-Beaulieu may define capital in whatever eccentric way he likes, but in common fairness let him not blame Marx for not using the word according to his definition.

On page 254, M. Leroy-Beaulieu allows the cloven hoof to come out which proves him to be in hopeless confusion as to the dialectical method on which the whole of the critical portion of the Kapital is based. Marx describes money "as the final product of the circulation of commodities" adding "this final product of the circulation of commodities is the first form of the appearance of Capital." This our eminent critic declares "inexact"

49

in the first place because "Capital," according to the Leroy-Beaulieu definition be it remembered, (which the prophetic spirit of Marx doubtless ought to have foreseen) can exist apart from money. (Our author had previously declared it possible to exist apart from exchange altogether, so that its existence apart from money must under these circumstances "go without saying.") We then read "Dans bien des sociétés l'usage de l'or et de l'argent dans les échanges est rélativement nouveau, au moins comme fait universel." Precisely; and this only proves that the principle enunciated by Marx is true no less historically than it is logically. The exactitude of Marx's proposition was never more concisely admitted.

The truth of the thesis that capital everywhere presents itself historically in opposition to land, as money in one or other of its forms, is conceded, but pronounced to have hardly any importance from an economical paint of view. We are not surprised that it should have little, in the eyes of the author of the present volume, although, as a matter of fact, it gives us the philosophic key to the whole economic problem. Land is necessarily opposed to money, inasmuch as they are separated by the whole universe of commodities. They are logically antithetical by a whole series of momenta. At the one extreme of the process is Land, as the formless Matter of the economic world, at the other Money, as its matterless form. Land is the infinite possibility of all economic things, as yet undetermined to anything in particular. Money on the other hand is the indefinite actuality of all such things, their determination as exchange-value. Between these two economically unreal extremes lies the real world of commodities for use, brought into being by the action of human labour on land or its natural products. Labour determines land or its products, gives it a specific and an individual form, in the commodity. The issue of the series of specific forms, ascending in complexity, is the money or pure form, which although possessing no specific content in itself, is the abstract expression for the whole world of commodities to which it has led up. This abstraction, like Almighty God according to Scotus Erigena, may best be defined as "pure nothing," from the real, i.e. the "utility" point of view. But as a matter of fact the Economists like the Theologians, have given their "pure-nothing" a local habitation and a name. Its name, too, is "Wonderful" "Counsellor," "Mighty God" (of the 19th century), the Everlasting Father (of the "self-made" Man), and (pace Mr. John Bright,) the "Prince of Peace." The abstract symbol or expression for exchange-value, money, acquires a fictitious reality in proportion as exchange-value itself dominates the world, in other words, as commodities are produced for exchange and not for use, and on this, be it remembered, does our capitalistic system rest.

The third chapter of the present work contains an impassioned homily on "Prescription," which is said to be the sole safeguard against universal war, &c. The idea of "prescription" is apparently introduced to screen the present possessors of landed property which was originally confiscated from ecclesiastical and public lands. As an argument against "nationalisation" it is however singularly inept. It applies a principle which, in our anarchical society rightly enough obtains as between one individual and another, to the relations of the individual to the community – a very different thing. The so-called "prescriptive right" simply means that mere possession gives a right to the individual possessing, as against any other individual, who cannot prove a greater right qua individual. But as against society, prescription has no existence. "Society gave and society taketh away; blessed be the name of Society."

As regards nationality, the principle of prescription is similar. So long as nationalism exists, each nation by virtue of established possession has the right to undisturbed enjoyment of its own territory as against any other nation. But once place politics on an international footing and it is evident one nation will not be able to plead prescription against any measure decided upon, by the European or the World-federation for the common good. So much for M. Leroy-Beaulieu's attempted assimilation of the principle of individual to that of national land-ownership. (see Chap. V)

We had noted many more things concerning M. Leroy-Beaulieu and his book for animadversion, but enough we think has been said to show its general character. Of course we have the stock arguments, that the capitalist is an organiser of labour, that the difficulties of direction and organisation in a Socialist State would be insuperable, that Mr. Giffen, who is described as a "statisticien très exact," says that the position of the working-classes is ameliorating, &c., &c. A great deal is made of the endeavour to prove that the "grief historique" of Marx is unfounded because, forsooth, it is possible to discover other subsidiary causes contributing to the origination of the accumulation of capital besides those leading ones mentioned by Marx. We would observe in conclusion that the case of Scientific Socialism must be indeed strong, when a leading French economist like M. Leroy-Beaulieu, after having taken in hand the case against it, cuts so sorry a figure.

E. Belfort Bax

Notes

1. Le Collectivisme. Examen critique du nouveau Socialisme, par Paul Leroy-Beaulieu, Membre de L'institut, &c., Paris Guillemin et Cie.

2. The above, of course, is an exposition in the abstract of the law of economic development. In the absence of other factors every society and, a fortiori, the

history of the world would follow precisely this course, just as in the absence of all resistance motion would pursue a straight line to infinity. But, as a matter of fact, in the concrete there are other elements present which retard, accelerate, or modify, this process at any particular stage. Ethical, religious, and political forms react upon the economical. Thus in the earliest civilisations of the world we find the religious element in the society dominating the whole; a hierarchy overlays the original basis, which while modifying it, preserves it from dissolution. In the classical period a partial individualism obtains in economics but is not yet reflected in Ethics or religion. In the period of the later Roman Empire, Individualism obtains in Ethics and religion, but the political hierarchy remains, and its forms are assimilated by the new ecclesiasticism (partly as a necessity of its existence). A new element now supervenes. The Germanic barbarians in full village community pour in. The Roman imperial order, and the hierarchy of the Church, the forms of both of which are indirectly traceable to the organisation of the early theocratic monarchies, were now met by simple primitive communism, Christian individualism remaining, in theory at least, the ethical basis of society. The fusion of these principles had as its result Catholic-feudal Europe. Now a complete Collectivism of society can never arise except out of one in which Individualism is completely worn out, i.e., in which it has completely prevailed not merely in Economics, but in Politics, Religion, and Ethics. In our modern society, for the first time in the world's history, this condition is realised. Individualist anarchy dominates in every department of human life. In the 16th century the mediaeval hierarchy was broken up. From that time forward Individualism has steadily extended its sway, and now reigns supreme. Hence it is that now, for the first time in the world's history, a Collectivist reconstruction becomes possible.

53

# Socialism and Religion
# (June 1884)

It is sometimes said that Socialism is neither religious nor irreligious. This does not or should not mean that Socialism fails to come into contact with the views of the world and of life which the current religions furnish, or that at a particular stage in its progress it may not take up a position even of active hostility to those religions. What it means is that Socialism implies a state of society out and away beyond the barren speculative polemics of the hour.

Socialism is essentially, neither religions nor irreligious, inasmuch as it re-affirms the unity of human life, abolishing the dualism which has lain at the foundation of all the great ethical religions. By this dualism I mean the antithesis of politics and religion, of the profane and the sacred, of matter and spirit, of this world and the "other world," and the various subordinate antagonisms to which these have given rise, or which they implicitly contain. Hitherto the whole tendency of our society and thought has been to make of aspects of things, distinguishable if you will, but not legitimately separable, separate and more or less opposed principles. We will take only the instance which most concerns the subject-matter of these remarks. The feelings, aspirations, emotions, (as we chose to call them), after the ideal, which constitute the "religious sentiment," are very easily distinguishable from the impulses of kindliness, friendship, duty, &c., to individuals which ought to animate our daily life. They are distinguishable but not separable. Yet the current religions erect them into distinct principles, severing the "religious sentiment" from all connection with the world and human society and transferring it to an imagined supernatural "world" which is nothing but a grotesque travesty of the relations of this world.

It is curious to trace how this came about. In the most ancient civilisations there is no distinction between the political or social and the religious, simply because religion was then nothing more than the propitiation of dead ancestors, powers of nature, fetiches or other supposed supernatural agents (whose existence passed unquestioned to the human mind in its then stage) in the interests of the society. These ancestral ghosts, personified powers, or animated fetiches were as often immoral as not, in fact it would be more correct to say that for them morality and immorality had no existence. The worshipper possibly cared not one jot for them or they for him – his worship was a social duty. The only way in which they possessed any human interest was as embodying certain powers, which might be noxious or beneficient to the State. We have spoken of them as being "propitiated" and "worshipped" but it is doubtful if those terms can he applied with regard to the ancient religious cults more than very partially. The practices they embodied were rather those of compulsory invocation or regulation by means of magical spells and incantations than prayers and "services" such as are understood to-day. The social festivals were as much religious as they were political. Political and religious functions were necessarily united in the same persons since every religions act was political, every political act also religious.

The forgoing remarks apply in all essentials, to every primitive civilisation, to ancient India, Egypt, China, Syria, Palestine. Even in later classical times, religion was still a social and political matter, a thing of this world only or mainly. The most sacred forms of the Greek and Roman cults were those identified with the preservation of the city, of the tribe and of the gens. Undoubting as was men's belief in the existence of the supernatural, it only interested them in so far as they conceived it

55

to affect the community of which they were a part. The supernatural too, was as yet imperfectly distinguished from the natural. There was no religion of the supernatural as such. But with the decay of the old civic morality and the absorption of the small free States into centralised monarchies and finally into the Roman Empire, men came to care less and less for the body politic and fell back more and more upon themselves as individuals. At first this individualism took the form of a search among the leisured and educated class for the higher life of wisdom. The Stoic, the Epicurean and the Cynic had each his special receipt for slipping through life as comfortably as possible. But this, though satisfactory for a time, palled in the long run. The Roman Empire got ever more corrupt, its corruption ramifying through all its branches; public life became more and more vapid; the old religions, once instinctive with meaning, were but empty forms; the newer panaceas of the philosophers failed to afford satisfaction. The utmost they promised was to make the best of the doubtful bargain – life.

But the sense of individualism was too strong for this merely negative creed. Men sought in vain for an object in life collective or individual. In this state of mind they are confronted by a new Asiatic sect. They become initiated. At once the scene changes. This life is indeed pronounced hopelessly worthless. There is no citizenship here, no happiness for the individual, not even the apathy of the "wise man." But as this life crumbles into nothingness, there rises the fair vision of the "city of God," joys beyond imagination, not the "apathy" of "wisdom," but the "peace" of the blest. Hic Rhodus hic salta! Religion is henceforth separated from life, the religious sphere of another world is set over against the irreligious sphere of this world. Earth is drained of its ideal to feed Heaven. Society established on this basis involves the antagonisms of temporal and spiritual powers, of "world" and church, of religious and profane, &c., &c. What is said applies not only to Christianity, but more or less to all the so-called ethical or universal religions, Zoroastrianism, Buddhism, Mohommedanism, &c.. They are the expression of the decay of the old life, and hence they one and all centre in the individual and in another world, their concern with this world being purely incidental.

We daily see around us the result of 1,600 years of "other-worldliness" on character and conduct. Men and women upon whom the mere greed for gain palls, are driven to the one ideal resource their education has given them, or they can comprehend, the hope of a glorified immortality for themselves. Those only who know from bitter experience the smile of honest contempt with which such people greet the idea of the sacrifice of personal or class privileges, or anything, else for a social object, can appreciate the depth to which the canker has eaten into their souls. Yet it would be unjust to say that these people are bad. They are religious and anti-social just as there are many others irreligious and anti-social.

In what sense Socialism is not religious will be now clear. It utterly despises the "other world" with all its stage properties – that is, the present objects of religion. In what sense it is not irreligious will be also I think tolerably clear. It brings back religion from heaven to earth, which as we have sought to show was its original sphere. It looks beyond the present moment or the present individual life indeed, though not to another world, but to another and higher social life in this world. It is in the hope and the struggle for this higher social life, ever-widening, ever-intensifying, whose ultimate possibilities are beyond the poorer of language to express or thought to conceive, that the Socialist finds his ideal, his religion. He sees in the reconstruction of society in the interest of all the rehabilitation, in a higher form and without its limitations, of the old communal life – the proximate end of all present endeavour. We take up the thread of

Aryan tradition, but not where it was dropped. The state or city of the ancient world was one-sided, its freedom was political merely, based on the slavery of the many; that of the future will be democratic and social. It was exclusive, the union within implied disunion without; the life of the future will be international, cosmopolitan in its scope. Finally the devotion of its members was connected with the existent supernatural belief and involved a cultus; the devotion of the member of the socialised community, like the devotion of all true Socialists today, will be based on science and involve no cultus. In this last point the religion of the Socialist differs from the Positivist. The Positivist seeks to retain the forms after the beliefs of which they are the expression have lost all meaning to him. The Socialist whose social creed is his only religion, requires no travesty of Christian rites to aid him in keeping his ideal before him.


In Socialism the current antagonisms are abolished, the separation between politics and religion has ceased to be, since their object-matter is the same. The highest feelings of devotion to the Ideal are not conceived as different in kind, much less as concerned with a different sphere; to the commoner human emotions, but merely as a diverse aspect of the same fact. The stimulus of personal interest no longer able to poison at its source all beauty all affection, all heroism, in short all that is highest in us; the sphere of government merged in that of industrial direction; the limit of the purely industrial itself ever receding as the applied powers of Nature lessen the amount of human drudgery required; Art and the pursuit of beauty and of truth ever covering the ground left free by the "necessary work of the world" – such is the goal lying immediately before us, such the unity of human interest and of human life which Socialism would evolve out of the clashing antagonisms, the anarchical individualism, religious and irreligious, exhibited in the rotting world of to-day – and what current religion can offer a higher ideal or a nobler incentive than this essentially human one.

E. Belfort Bax

# Socialism and the Sunday Question
# (August 1884)

The question of a "free" Sunday is to no one more immediately important than to Socialists. For a proletariat strong in mind and in body is the first essential to the advent and the success of the revolution in this country as in every other. And no proletariat can be strong in mind or in body which is debarred from the opportunities of the full culture of either. The middle-class employer knows this right well when he protests against any infringement of the "day of rest." It was M. Guizot, so far as we remember, who in conversation with an English statesman sometime during the year 1848, remarked that the safety of England lay in its Sunday. Allowing for exaggeration, there is much truth in this assertion of the typical middle-class statesman of France. The "safety" of England, from the point of view of its privileged classes, has undoubtedly been conducted to by the British "Beer and Bible" Sunday. A well-conducted English workman, "thrifty and industrious," is no doubt, kept in a state of dogged contentment by never knowing what leisure intelligently occupied means, by his tastes being carefully kept under, and by his weekly holiday being "empty, swept, and garnished," of all relaxation. A man who knows nothing to interest him when he is free from work, naturally cares less about reduction of labour. It is culture in its widest sense which makes the revolutionist. By culture we do not mean the mere tools of education furnished by the School Board, but the habit of mind which forces a man beyond the here and the now of his own particular interests or even of the events uppermost in the newspapers at the moment and makes him feel a living interest and part, in the past, the future, the distant. Now it is the absence of culture in this sense which makes the English working classes safe and politically stable. While the French or German workman is occupied with "theories of the reorganisation of society," the English workman is content to keep his nose to the grindstone, heaping up, may be, a little competence for his old age, and, when political, to concern himself with "practical measures for the improvement of his class."

That the English Sunday is largely responsible for this state of affairs, we repeat, there is little doubt. But how came the Anglo-Saxon Sunday to be what it is? In mediaeval times, the Sunday was a day of recreation, of fairs, morris-dances, mystery plays, &c., and not of enforced idleness and gloom. The Puritan movement which originated at the end of the sixteenth century in the reign of Elizabeth, gathering force and numbers till the rebellion which cost Charles I his head, embodied in its programme a strong antagonism to the old English Sunday, an antagonism which was accentuated, by the action of the opposite party who took an equally emphatic stand upon the Sunday of tradition. There was nothing merely arbitrary in the position adopted on either side. It was the extreme carrying out of what was involved in the respective attitudes of both parties. The Puritan movement was essentially a movement of the English middle-class, the yeomanry of the country, and the guildsmen of the town as against the remains of the mediaeval aristocratic and church system. The attempt of Charles I to strengthen his prerogative – the shipmoney, the five members – only brought the crisis to an issue; its causes lay far deeper. Protestantism, the new middle-class version of Christianity, and Puritanism, the insular commentary on this version, abolished the festivals of Catholicism which had given the people well-nigh as many additional holidays in the year as there were Sundays. These old festival days here now dedicated to work, and although all work was vigorously interdicted on the Sabbath, so also was all pleasure. This beautiful conception of a "day of rest" was ratified by a Puritan Parliament in the well-known Act of Charles II. Thenceforward the English Sunday became the dreary day it is now.[1]

That it originated in the religious side of the English middle-class revolution of the 17th century does not mean that it has interfered with the material interests of the middle-class. Their zeal for the maintenance of the day as a "day of rest" does not imply the disinterestedness which at first sight might, be supposed. More than a certain amount of work in a year cannot be got out of the "human machine." Thus, where, as on the continent, there is no religious or legal hindrance to Sunday labour the weekly holiday is obtained in the great industries just the same nevertheless, either on Sundays as in France, or where as in Austria, labour is the rule on that day, on Monday – blue Monday as it is called. Now whether the leisure (which, the employer is forced to concede) be sacrificed on the altar of middle-class creed, or be employed for purposes of recreation or of instruction does not directly affect the pocket of the capitalist. But though it does not directly affect him, it does so very much indirectly, as the English middle-classes have found out. The man who through lack of something else to do is induced to interest himself in the administration of a Baptist chapel, is not so likely to be guilty of the middle-class sin of discontent as the man who uses his leisure otherwise. And such a man is the ideal workman of the British manufacturer.

To sum up the historical and actual aspects of the question. In the Middle Ages and indeed until production for profit became the motive power of the world's life, religion secured at least a fourth of the year in real holidays for the people; while for the rest, the Catholic Church, which was the conservator of the amusements as it was of the learning of the time, often interposed with effect to protect the serf from overwork. This was the case in England, as elsewhere, before the middle-class rising of 1649, subsequent to which, the religious aspect of the middle-class struggle in its crudest form, viz., Puritanism, the cardinal doctrine of which is the sinfulness of pleasure, suppressed the catholic fête-days of the old "merry England" as well as the traditional an amusements of Sunday. This arrangement has proved so conducive to order and good government that the institution of the British "Sabbath" has rightly come to be regarded as one of the bulwarks of capitalistic "order" in these islands. The twaddle talked abort the "Sabbath" protecting the workman from exaction is seen in its true light when we find that capitalism, in the long run, Sabbath or no Sabbath, is compelled to concede one day's holiday in the week; and that the only difference is as to what day it shall be and how that day shall be spent: points which the dominant classes in this county arrogate to themselves the right of deciding.

In conclusion we would wish to point out what in our view is the true solution of the Sunday – or rather rest-day – question. And in this we claim to be speaking strictly within the range of "practical politics," and not from a more advanced standpoint; for in a perfectly organised socialist state where men never worked more than two or three hours a day, the whole question would lose much of its interest and would practically solve itself. Now the fallacy which underlies the whole rationalistic defence for the English Sunday is the assumption that the whole world must rest on the same day if the whole world is to rest at all. This absurd notion of one universal holiday as the only alternative to none, is visible in the modern English equivalent for the mediaeval festivals of St. Peter and St. Paul, to wit, that dedicated to the supreme deity or patron saint of exchange, the Bank. Even here, the tendency is for the whole machinery of labour to cease at once, while on Sunday this actually takes place as far as possible. Now, I ask, could anything well be more irrational or more senseless than such a proceeding? It is obvious, if leisure is to be enjoyed usefully as regards mind or body some portion of the community must labour to enable the

63

rest to profit by their holiday. Horrible injustice! shriek the quondam humanitarian defenders of the British Sunday in chorus, you would make others work on the "day of rest" for your pleasure! I answer we would give every single worker at least one day of rest a week a blessing which a good many do not enjoy now (for all your English "Sabbath") and cannot in the nature of things enjoy, do what you may, while all are supposed to rest on the same day. But we would surrender once and for all this chimerical notion of one day of universal rest, and institute three days a week, or if necessary more, as; days of partial rest; i.e., on which the different sections of he community would be freed from labour in turn. In this way each section would be able rely to profit, physically and mentally, by their leisure, inasmuch as they would have the advantage of the labour of the rest of the world just as another day the rest of the world would have the advantage of their labour. Thus the "Sabbath" with its gloom would be for ever abolished and the weekly, or if you will, bi-weekly, holiday could be made a day of real enjoyment for all.

E. Belfort Bax

## Notes

1. Puritanism the insular guise of the larger movement of Protestantism which was the religious aspect of middle-class domination, formally abolished the outward relation of religion to daily-life. Under Catholicism, the old pagan feeling of the unity of human interests still survived, neither work nor amusement were altogether dissociated from religion. Puritanism finally separated them, and the Puritan Sunday in which all work and amusement are alike impious as an expression of this separation.

# Conscience and Commerce
# (November 1885)

WE often come across a species of virtuous indignation which is apt to be aroused by some tale of the woes of a railway company whom the wicked passenger "defrauds" by travelling, without having, previously paid his fare. "Strange," it is said (and we find the sentiment commonly repeated whenever the subject comes up in the Press), "that a man who would scorn to rob his neighbour in his individual capacity, yet will not hesitate to 'defraud' a company;" for it is acknowledged to be by such persons that the bulk of these "frauds" (so-called) are perpetrated. The inconsistency of such a proceeding is then enlarged upon with all due emphasis.

This in itself, comparatively unimportant incident of modern life, opens up a curious ethico-economical problem. Two things are quite clear. One is that a considerable section of persons instinctively feel a difference between their moral relations to individual men and women and their relations to a joint-stock company. The other is that the ordinary middle-class intellect cannot see any reason for this distinction, and having possibly a sense of the instability to commercial relations which would ensue from its recognition, adopts the high moral tone. Yet it is doubtful if even the most hardened bourgeois does not really feel that there is a difference between stealing a neighbour's coat and "defrauding" a joint-stock company, unwilling as he may be to acknowledge it.

Now the question is on what is this feeling of distinction based. It must have some explanation. We may as well state at once our conviction that it is based on the fact that in the one case there is a real moral relation involved, while in the other there is only a fictitious one – a fact which inherited moral instinct recognises, but, the reason sophisticated by the economic forms of modern society and the artificial morality necessary to them, refuses to admit.

We do not intend entering upon any elaborate discussion on the basis of ethics. But we suppose that every one will concede that the essence of moral relation is that it is between concretes – between one concrete individual and another, or else between that individual and the concrete social organism of which he forms a part. It is plain we cannot owe a duty either to an inanimate object or to an abstraction, as such. We speak, it is true, of "duty to the cause," but this is only a metaphor; we really mean duty to the oppressed humanity of to-day, and to the free society of the future, of which we are the pioneers. and which the "cause" represents. Furthermore, all ethical relations between individuals involve reciprocity – they imply a mutual obligation, a personal responsibility on either side. In the Middle Ages all relations in life were directly or indirectly personal in their character. The feudal relation was eminently a personal one. The mercantile relation, in so far as it existed, was a personal one. Now the sense of honour, honesty, etc., both logically and historically, has meaning alone in connection with a personal relation. Peter as an individual has certain definite moral relations to Paul, amongst others that of respecting his belongings, in so far as appropriation for personal use is concerned.[1] This is a relation as between man and man. He owes the obligation to Paul as a concrete individual, not to Paul's coat, or his money. Paul, on the other hand, has identical obligations towards Peter. There is personal responsibility on either side. Again, the individual has plain duties towards the community, in so far as property designed for its use is concerned. (Of course, I am all along dealing with our present society.) He as an individual is bound to

66

respect the belongings of the public; for instance, not to appropriate prints or books from the British Museum, not to destroy pictures in the National Gallery, not to steal commons or to "restore" ancient monuments (in which last, two particulars, since they do not threaten the stability of Capitalism, the bourgeois conscience is more elastic than in the matter of "defrauding" companies). Here, also, the relation is between concretes – between a definite personality and a definite community. The picture, books, commons, monuments are (or are supposed to be) there for the use and enjoyment of the community, and the community suffers a wrong in their destruction or alienation.

But to return to our Peter and Paul. We have said that the moral relation of Peter and Paul rests on a basis of reciprocal personal responsibility and on this alone. It was on such a basis that the feeling of honour in the dealings of life had its rise and in this alone it has any meaning. There was a relation of mutual personal obligation between the feudal lord and the vassal or serf. That the lord often neglected his obligation does not alter the fact of its existence. There was a personal relation between buyer and seller, master and workman, and indeed in every sphere of life in the old time and in simpler conditions of society. But with the rise of Capitalism the personal relation has fallen into the background, personal responsibility has been allowed to lapse to an ever-increasing extent before the exigencies of modern competitive conditions of industry. The responsible proprietor of a business detaches himself more and more as a personality from his business. The name over the door may or may not be his own name, but anyway he obliterates his personality as far as may be by the addition of the words "& Co." You plead with such a man for some act of grace to a creditor or employé; "business is business," will be his reply, a reply which surely enough indicates the impersonal, anti-social methods of Commercialism. In pursuit of its object, individual gain, Commercialism abstracts the

67

individual from his personality. The modern capitalist lives a dual life; as capitalist he ceases more and more to be man. Private relations and business relations tend to become more and more abstracted from one another. Yet our capitalist forgets that it is only as man, as a concrete personality, that he can justly claim moral obligations from his fellow-men. If as the "head of a firm" he stands in any moral relation to other personalities, it is only by virtue of the fact that the divorce between his manhood and his "headship of the firm" is incomplete, that the personal relation is not altogether abolished. His belongings as "head of the firm" are to be respected, because even under this disguise he is recognised as a thing of flesh and blood.

But there is one form under which modern capitalism functions – its most advanced form – in which the last shred of personal responsibility is torn from its operations. We refer to what the French aptly call the societé anonyme – that thing without a name, the joint-stock company. Here at last is naked capital, the last shred of its human covering gone – capital without a capitalist – the thing of which the proverb says, it has "neither soul to save, nor heart to feel, nor body to kick." The abstraction is now complete, but at the same moment transformed into a hyperphysical, hyperethical entity. With the "head of the firm" there is always the chance (though possibly a faint one) that the man may get the better of the capitalist human feelings may even hold back the demon "business" – the possibility of conscience is there to which to make your appeal. But here there is nothing but surplus-value. Fancy has imagined beings composed of water or of fire merely – Undines and Salamanders. Here is a being composed of the "circulating process of capital." By dint of the power of money the widow and orphan are ruined by litigation, are driven from court to court in search of their just and obvious claims. Employés of long-standing service are turned off at a week's notice when not wanted. You appeal to the conscience of the secretary, the manager, the director, against these enormities. The reply is simple: "We are here merely to look after the interests of the shareholders"; which, being interpreted, means, having duly appropriated the customary "pickings," to see that as much profit as possible is wrung out, of "servants" and "public" regardless of all other considerations. But how about these shareholders? Peter, let us say, is a shareholder. He is one of those who has deliberately merged a certain amount of his property (his belongings) in an impersonal abstraction, over the working of which he has practically no control. He has severed this portion of his belongings from his concrete individuality. It is a quantum of circulating capital abstracted from the man. The "company" consists entirely in a sum-total of such quanta of capital. The holder is merely an accident, both qualitatively and quantitatively. The sum-total of these quanta of capital may be "held" indifferently by twenty men or twenty thousand. They may be clever or stupid, humane or criminal. As personalities they are utterly indifferent. Peter, though a shareholder, is in his relation to the working of the "company" but as one of the "ordinary public." The member of a trade-firm is personally responsible (more or less) for the working of that firm. Not so here. The man – the capitalist, if you will – has altogether abstracted his "belongings" from that to which they belong – from himself. It matters not what action may be taken in the name of the "company," he, the private shareholder, is powerless to prevent it. Once in it, the ghastly Frankenstein may dance on his Conscience, and beyond an impotent protest he can do nothing. "But he can sell out," you will say. Of what avails it? The action goes on: he has only shifted the nominal responsibility from his own shoulders to his neighbours. The "company" remains. Holders come and holders go, but shares flow on for ever. The company is constituted essentially of the shares, and only accidentally of the men that hold them.

In what relation, then, does the individual – concrete man

or woman – the thing of flesh and blood, stand to this abstraction? We have taken for granted as indisputable that we cannot stand in a moral relation to an abstraction or an inanimate object or indeed to anything but a concrete sentient being. We cannot owe a duty to Peter's coat or his money but only to Peter. We cannot, therefore, stand in any real moral relation to the Joint-stock company. But the interests of Commercialism require that the wholly impersonal jointstock company like the semi-personal business "firm," should be treated to all practical intents and purposes as though it were a full living human personality. In law of course he has the full rights of personality. In morality it has stolen them, or tried to steal them. It claims (tacitly if not explicitly) in the name not only of law but of honour forsooth, a claim to make the gods laugh, respect for its "property" and the fulfilment of a bargain which it tacitly assumes the individual to be bound by when he takes advantage of the social function it casually performs (more or less badly) in pursuit of its sole end, the extraction of the greatest possible amount of profit from producer and consumer. The sacred name of "honour" and "honesty" originating in far other conditions of society, and implying reciprocal obligations, is prostituted by the modern bourgeois mind to facilitate the "trickstering" and "profit-grinding" of modern competitive commerce for which on its own side moral obligations do not exist or exist at best on sufferance. But a suspicion of the instability of the title of the joint-stock company to be treated as a moral personality pierces the legal and conventional fiction. A waft of healthy moral instinct whispers to a man that it is not the same thing to "defraud" a "company" as to rob his neighbour. But he does not know how to justify his instinctive impression. Hence when brought to book he cries a mea culpa. It is only the student of social evolution to whom the bogus nature of the title by which the "Joint-stock" company, and to a lesser extent of that by which other forms of "commercial" individuality, impudently lay claim to recognition as object of moral obligation, is revealed in all its clearness.

The "Slocum-Mudford railway company;" let us suppose, appeals to the honour of the individual passenger not to prejudice its interests by "fraud" or otherwise. "But," says the individual, "who are you? I as a moral man recognise my duty to all other persons individually as well as to the community as a whole. But you are neither an individual nor the community, and I decline to admit that I have any duties in your case at all. 'Peter I know, and Paul I know, but who are you?' My conscience does not respond to your appeal. It strikes me, on the contrary, that you and your congeners are fitting subjects for the free exercise of those free individualist tendencies about which the salaried defenders of the state of society which gives you birth wax so eloquent. 'Business is business;' let us have no sentimentality. We are on a footing of competition, only that, it is not 'free,' seeing that you have the law on your side. However, let that bide. Your 'business' is to get as much money-value as possible out of me the passenger on your line ('conveyance' being the specific form of social utility your capital works in, in order to realise itself as surplus value) and to give as little as possible in return, only in fact so much as will make your line pay. My 'business,' as an individual passenger, on the contrary, is to get as much use-value, to derive as much advantage from the social function which you casually perform in pursuance of your profit, as I possibly can, and to give you as little as possible in return. You seek under the protection of the law to guard yourself from 'fraud,' as you term it. Good. If I can evade the law passed in your interest and elude your vigilance, I have a perfect right to do so, and my success in doing so will be the reward of my ingenuity. If I fail I am only an unfortunate man. The talk of 'dishonesty' or 'dishonour' where no moral obligation or 'duty' can possibly exist is absurd. You choose to make certain arbitrary rules to regulate the commercial game. I decline to pledge myself to be bound by them, and in so doing I am clearly within my moral right. We each try to get as much out of the other as we can, you in your way, I in mine.

71

Only, I repeat, you are backed by the law, I am not. That is all the difference."


The question with which we set out has now been answered. We took an extreme instance to start with, but our explanation covers the whole range of similar phenomena; for instance, the distinction felt between a "debt of honour" and a tradesman's bill. In the commercial relation as such the moral relation is abolished. In proportion as the personality, with its human responsibility, retreats into the background, leaving us confronted with the lifeless, bloodless vampire. Trade, by so much do the words "duty," "honour", "morality," lose meaning. "Conscience," which has its ground in social union, can have no part, nor lot with "Commerce," which has its ground in anti-social greed. But the transition from the personal or conscientious to the purely commercial relation is so gradual and is complicated by so many other factors, that it is quite easy for the bourgeois mind to keep up the fiction that honour or dishonour can be involved even in dealing with that commercial abstraction, the "joint-stock company." A general recognition of the sham claim of commercial abstractions to moral consideration, could not but prove embarrassing to the modern commercial system, which would then have to rely on its legal defences alone.


## Notes

1. It is necessary to make this last caveat, as of course every Socialist will admit the justifiability of the community's confiscating individual wealth to public purposes, and of course any one individual might be the agent of this confiscation in any particular case.

# Unscientific Socialism
# (January 1884)

In the exposition of a subject such as Socialism, as in the rebuilding of an edifice, there is a preliminary stage of destructive activity. Old material, in the one case, has to be carted away, and the ground to be generally dug up and cleared. In the other, we have similarly to clear out intellectual ground of theories likely to interfere with our contemplated structure. Now, no material is so much in danger of cumbering us as that which superficially resembles our own, but is in reality old and rotten. In the following remarks I propose to examine briefly four codes of ideas (for theories or systems they cannot all of them be called) which are nominally socialistic, and profess certain principles in. common with socialism proper, but are, nevertheless, essentially distinct from it. These four codes of ideas are: I. Christian Socialism, so called; II. An indefinite kind of awakening to social imperfections among the youth of the middle classes to which I give the name Sentimental Socialism; III. The various social schemes propounded, and in part sought to be carried out in various parts of North America, dating from the earlier half of the nineteenth century, to which the general name of Utopian Socialism is commonly applied; and IV. Anarchism.

The Christian Socialism with which we are here concerned is not the imperial-Bismarckic device known by that name in Germany which to English readers, at least, is too transparent to need criticism, but a more insidious, because more honest, attempt to pour new wine into old bottles. A body of High churchmen, calling themselves the Guild of St. Matthew, held a series of meetings towards the close of last year, for the discussion of this Christian Socialism. It was difficult to obtain any very clear notion of what Christian Socialism meant from the ideas set forth by its professed exponents, even apart from the want of unanimity displayed.. But to judge from most of the opening addresses, as well as from an explanatory letter published subsequently by the. Rev. Canon Shuttleworth, what was understood as the practical basis of Christian Socialism, is trade co-operation or industrial partnership, such as has from time to time been carried out, and of which the Decorators' Co-operative Association is an example. This is significantly confirmed by the fact that the worthy canon, when asked at the close of his address in proof of an assertion he had made to furnish the names of any Socialistic leaders who could, in any sense, be described as Christian, against the long array of anti-Christian names, from Marat and Baboeuf to Lassalle and Marx, which were cited against him, could only bring forward those of the astute capitalist-co-operators Leclaire and Godin, as historical evidence of the independent existence of the Christian Socialist. It was undoubtedly some scheme of co-operation, we may observe, that the "old", "original" Christian Socialists in this country, Kingsley and Maurice, had in view.

Now, a very little reflection suffices to show us that all such schemes are not only within the lines of the current bourgeois system of ideas, habits, and aspirations, but that they reflect that system in some of its worst aspects. As to the shrewd philanthropist Leclaire, the co-operator's "great man," verily he was not without his capitalistic reward, leaving, as he did, a fortune of £48,000 behind him. But personal questions apart, on entering one of these co-operative establishments what is the first thing that greets the eye? A list of "regulations," if anything more stringent than those of an ordinary workshop, indicating longer hours and harder work. The principle underlying these institutions would seem to be that the supreme end of life is the maximisation of labour, and the minimisation of the enjoyment of its product. "Labour," or "industry," (as it might probably be

74

termed) seems to be regarded by co-operators as one of those good things of which it is impossible to have too much. As a consequence they are jealous of all time spent otherwise than in labour, i.e. manufacture of commodities, and are averse to the consumption or enjoyment of the product of such labour as at once a loss of time and a waste of material which would otherwise be saved. Now all this may be very nice, but so far from being Socialism, it is the very antithesis of Socialism. Trade co-operation is simply a form of industrial partnership, in which the society of co-operators is in the relation of capitalist to the outer world. The units of the society may be equal amongst themselves (always excepting the broken-down capitalist who is the presiding genius, the Leclaire or Godin), but their very existence in this form pre-supposes exploitation going on above, below and around them, in other words the prevailing industrial anarchy.

As I have said, co-operative experiments reflect what are, from a Socialistic point of view, the worst aspects of the current order. The trade co-operator canonises the bourgeois virtues, but Socialist vices, "over-work," and "thrift." To the Socialist, labour is an evil to be minimised to the utmost. The man who works at his trade or avocation more than necessity compels him, or who accumulates more than he can enjoy, is not a hero but a fool from the Socialist's standpoint. It is this necessary work which it is the aim of Socialism to reduce to the minimum. Again, "thrift," the hoarding up of the products of labour, it is obvious must be without rhyme or reason, except on a capitalist basis. For the only two purposes which commodities serve are consumption and exchange. Now except under peculiar circumstances (arctic expeditions and the like), it is certain they would not be "saved" to any considerable extent merely for the sake of future consumption. Hence the object of "thrift," or hoarding, must lie in exchange. And, in short, it is the increment obtainable by commodities or realised labour-power when represented by

75

exchange-value or money, that furnishes the only raison d'etre of "thrift." The aim of the Socialist, therefore, which is the enjoyment of the products of labour as opposed to that of the bourgeois which is their mere accumulation with a view to "surplus-value" is radically at variance with "thrift."

Having shown that in so far as it has any defined economic basis at all, "Christian Socialism" is anti-socialistic, it might seem hardly necessary to criticise it further, but as a matter of fact the whole scheme is so vague and intangible, that it is quite possible some persons may really believe in the accomplishment of vast changes (whether the modus operandi be the expropriation of competition rents, or what not) of a really socialistic nature through the instrumentality of a clarified Christianity, a Christianity which shall consist apparently of the skins of dead dogmas stuffed with an adulterated Socialist ethics, and of formulas which though to the simple mind they seem plain enough, the brotherhood of the Guild of St. Matthew will show us mean something quite different from what they seem.

In justice it must be said, that the Ritualistic priests we are here criticising, exhibit a generosity and a charity which they may call Christian, but which seem to us very much better than anything in the way of those commodities we have seen produced by Christianity outside the Guild of St. Matthew. There is, however, one thing that appears to ruffle the usually equable temper even of these gentlemen, and that is, to be confronted with any definite dogma, text, or formula. Not that we have ever found them at a loss to explain away the irrational and immoral in such into something perfectly harmless, rational, moral, and worthy of all acceptation, when called upon to do so, but they, nevertheless, appear to think such things as recognised Christian doctrines quite irrelevant even when the possibility of such a combination as Christian Socialism is in question. Our Neo-

Christian friends may, without any special inconsistency, refuse to be saddled with "Semitic myths," or may even contend, as did Canon Shuttleworth, that the Christianity they profess is independent of the Canonical Hebrew Scriptures considered as a whole. But surely they at least must be prepared to stand by the accepted character and teaching of their titular founder. It is surely fair to confront them with this. Now it is upon the ground of the traditional character and teaching that we are prepared to join issue with them when they assert its Socialistic nature. We can readily understand the charm it exercises on certain minds. We know that inherited tendencies, upbringing, and the like, all conduce in sensitive natures to clothe with the rich and glowing hues of their own beauty and emotion, a shadowy figure, in which those who have divested themselves of those tendencies, and view things with the colder eye of impartiality, see at best a weak but impulsive personality. But it is only natural that these latter should resent with some indignation the continual reference of ideal perfection to a semi-mythical Syrian of the first century, when they see higher types even in some now walking this upper earth, but in vulgar flesh and blood, and without the atmosphere of nineteen centuries to lend enchantment to them. How many such are there not and have there not been in the modern Socialist movement who do their work, give up their all, without posing as Messiahs, but choosing rather the nobler part of sinking their individuality in their cause?

As to the ethical teaching of Christ with its one-sided, introspective and individualistic character, we venture to assert that no one acquainted with the theory of modern scientific Socialism can for one moment call it Socialistic. Socialism aims rather at a rehabilitation (in a higher form) of the classical utilitarian morality of public life. It has no sympathy with the hysterical eternally-revolving-in-upon-itself transcendent morality of the gospel discourses. This morality, like that of the whole Oriental movement of which it is a development, is

77

essentially subjective, its criterion lying in the individual conscience, and its relation to a divinity supposed to reveal himself in it. It sets up a forced, to the vast majority, impossible standard of "personal holiness," which, when realised, has seldom resulted in anything but (1) an apotheosised priggism (e.g. the puritan type), or (2) in an epileptic hysteria (e.g. the catholic saint type), and which at the best is a tour-de-force involving an amount of concentrated moral energy that may excite our wonder perhaps, just as may the concentrated physical energy of the tight-rope dancer, but which we feel to be just as useless. But if it is useless in those exceptional cases where attained, it is worse than useless, in its effects on the generality of men. With Christian asceticism as the ethical standard which all good men are supposed to attain, but which as a matter of fact no good man really thinks of attaining, men are driven to the compromise of pretending to attain it. It is thus that hypocrisy arises. In the classical world hypocrisy was all but unknown. Aristotle, in his elaborate analysis of virtues and vices in the Ethics, hardly alludes to it. It was born of the Oriental-introspective ethics of Christianism, and with their establishment in Europe it took its place as an integral factor of social life. This has been more than ever the case since the triumph of its most purely individualist form in Protestantism. The success of Christianity as a moral force has been solely upon isolated individuals. In its effect on societies at large, it has signally and necessarily failed. Though Socialism has no sympathy with anti-Semitism as generally understood, it certainly represents the assertion of the Aryan ethics (whether classical or Norse) of social utility as against the Semitic ethics of personal holiness – (I say the Semitic ethics since the so-called Christian ethic was no more the discovery of Jesus than of Hillel, of Philo, or of any other individual, but like all great movements and discoveries, was the result of the concentrated thought of generations).

The brotherhood of the Guild of St. Matthew merely

78

represents a phase common to ages of transition in which the reactionary ideal and morality endeavours to steal a march on the progressive ideal and morality. The modern broad-High church, or eclectic movement in Christendom offers an exact analogy to the eclectic movement in Paganism of the 3rd and 4th centuries AD. In either a modus vivendi is sought to be effected between the immorality and absurdity of the popular theology, Pagan or Christian, and the growing aspirations of the earnest and thoughtful. And the manner in which this is done is no less analogous. The whole external structure of dogma, legend, and ceremonial is retained, not a tittle of it is repudiated while it is carefully emptied of all its original and obvious meaning, and by a dexterous ingenuity forced to represent something which neither "Christian, Pagan, nor man" ever dreamt of its representing before.

Any attempt at mutilating or defacing the exterior of a creed or cultus is always unsuccessful. The purification of Paganism sought to be effected by the Epicureans and earlier Platonists through the rejection of the legends of the poets and popular traditions respecting the gods, and the shearing down of ceremonial, touched only a section of the cultured. The only even temporarily successful clarified Paganism was that represented by Plotinus, Porphyry, Julian, and Proclus, which held every legend and ceremonial sacred, while reading into them the Oriental ethics then becoming popular. Similarly, the barren ceremonial and unsymmetrical theology of Unitarianism has never had any success save among a limited section of the middle-classes. Taking these facts into consideration, to wit, that symmetry of creed and taste in ritual count for much in human nature and in the popularity of a cultus, the move made by the Guild of St. Matthew and similar associations is strategically not a bad one, from the standpoint of clericalism. But its achievement of even the temporary success of the Neo-Platonists (which was owing in great measure to causes not now in operation) is more than doubtful. The working-classes see plainly enough that Christianity in all its forms belongs to a civilisation of the past and of the present, but not that civilisation of the future which signifies their emancipation.

The sentimental Socialist, though not necessarily Christian, retains essentially the introspective attitude of the Christian ethics. He forms societies, the members of which are supposed to pledge themselves to indefinitely high aims, aims that tower above the clouds from which it requires the practised eye to distinguish them. These aims "won from the void and formless infinite" seem to be only won for the sake of being handed over to the equally formless indefinite. The only shape approaching articulation into which they wreath themselves, is that of resolutions and letters. The young people of the well-to-do middle-class, for whom sentimental Socialism possesses attractions, think human nature susceptible of higher aims than the current ones, and meet in drawing rooms for the apparent purpose of passing resolutions to that effect. The sentimental Socialist desires above all things to be broad and comprehensive. Now any proposition conveying a distinct meaning is necessarily limited by that meaning, and must be taken to exclude its opposite, and a fortiori the society adopting it to exclude those who hold its opposite. But how can a society whose aims are so high, condescend to such small matters of detail as meaning? How can a man as catholic as the "Brother of the Higher Life," or the member of the "Communion of Noble Aspirations," or the New Atlantis Society be so narrow as to exclude any one. Hence in the resolutions adopted by such associations, the first requisite is the absence of meaning. All is possible in the man (or woman) who aims high enough., Danton's motto "to dare, to dare, and again to dare," becomes in the hands of the sentimental Socialist, "to aim, to aim, and again to aim" at an ineffable O – Voilà tout. All this "casting of empty buckets into empty wells and drawing nothing up" may be entertaining, beautiful, ennobling for a short spell, but palls after a time, which is probably the explanation of the fact that these societies that start so rosy bright invariably die of inanition within measurable distance of their inauguration, though only to make way for new ones. The young men and women of our blasé middle-class civilisation require a stimulus; this stimulus may be aesthetic, philanthropic, or social. It may consist in languishing vapouring on art, on improved dwellings, on social reconstruction. Just now it wears the latter aspect. The whole movement is born of the morbid self-consciousness of our Christian and Bourgeois civilisation run to seed.

The Utopian Socialist schemes of the first half of the present century, which are conveniently brought forward by the votaries of the current bourgeois economy as a dummy to be battered down, under the pretence of demolishing Socialism proper, stand condemned ab initio, owing to their lack of a scientific basis. These attempts bear the same relation to modern scientific Socialism that astrology or alchemy do to astronomy and chemistry. The attempt of Goethe's Wagner to construct a homunculus artificially was scarcely more preposterous than those of Owen, Fourier, or St. Simon to construct a society artificially. It is as rational to introduce Owen, Fourier, &c., with their "New Harmonies" and phalansteries, into discussions on scientific Socialism as it would be to introduce Paracelsus or Van Helmont, with their lilies and roses, into discussions on chemistry. Utopian Socialism was only the pre-scientific and infantile stage of that matured Science of society which modern Socialism represents on its practical side. Yet there are people who still believe in (more or less) select little bands going into the backwoods and founding colonies, undeterred by the numberless wrecks of shattered hopes they see around them. No experiment of this kind, as might be expected, has had (even avowedly) any other than a Christian or sentimental basis. Most of the so-called communistic societies of the United States are really nothing more than religious sects, which have found it

81

convenient to come out of the world. They have really no more right to the special appellation "Socialist" than a body of monks.


Of course, in a sense, any monastic society may be termed communistic, inasmuch as its members practise, like the early Christians, or the Essenes, a certain primitive communism or community of goods. And in this sense of course the erratic protestant sects of the United States – the Shakers, the Perfectionists, the Separatists, &c. – who have formed themselves into similar independent communities on a somewhat larger scale, may be termed communistic or socialistic. Otherwise the term Socialist has no meaning as applied to them, least of all in the modern scientific sense of the word in which Socialism is regarded as the result of a transformation of the existent conditions of society throughout the civilised world, and to which therefore any "coming out of the world," in the sense of establishing an independent "community of saints" is an anachronism. Socialism proper, presupposes the developed industrial system, the machinery, the population &c., of the most advanced countries of modern times as its essential antecedent condition, and whether right or wrong, true or false, takes its stand on the continuity of historic evolution. It is no Utopian scheme or theory of what a model society might be, but claims to be a deduction of what the outcome of our present capitalistic civilisation itself must be sooner or later, unless social evolution is to be arrested by dissolution. (Political economists who interpolate chapters on "Communism" or "Socialism" into their treatises, please take note).


The last point referred to, brings us to the question Anarchism. Now the Anarchist frankly accepts the alternation of dissolution. He desires no reorganisation. He is a logical, thorough-going individualist – none of your sham bourgeois individualists, whose conception of individual liberty is the liberty of themselves and their class to "exploit" those below them without restriction, under the guise of freedom of contract – but an individualist whose conceptions of individual liberty is absolute for each and all, and knows no distinction. The Anarchist would resolutely destroy all organisation whatever, however salutary. He would resolve society into its component units – in other words, as we said, his goal is social dissolution. Every bond of social union would be severed, each individual "free to make 'little hell' for himself," as Mr. Hyndman has it. Our first criticism on this is that disintegration such as the Anarchist aims at, even if brought about, could hardly endure for a day. The social organism, in its present stage is analogous to those low biological organisms which, subdivided as you will, re-combine and reorganise by their very nature and that of the medium in which they exist. The result of any violent disintegration, if successful, that is, if the whole of the bourgeois civilisation of to-day were entirely destroyed – rather than transformed or changed into a new and higher civilisation, which is what the Collectivist aims at – would simply recombine on lines belonging to a lower stage of the old economic development, the old society would reform, but at the point arrived at fifty years ago or more, and the whole intervening period, or something similar would have to be gone over again. This is the utmost that would be achieved. The social organism is as yet in too low a stage to be more than temporarily deranged in its development by any violence that could be done it. A violent dissolution – were this possible, a point we do not argue – would be speedily followed by reintegration on the old lines.

We have, of course, merely referred to the possibility of the permanence of Anarchism, and have said nothing as to the desirability of the destruction of those elements of the current civilisation, bought by the bitter toil and experience of centuries of human effort, which, though under the present organisation of society, they merely serve for the enslavement of the greater portion of mankind, under a higher organisation might be the means of their emancipation from the bondage of toil, and of affording the possibility of comfort, art, and culture for each and all. The struggle between man and nature – including that which is natural, i.e., merely animal and brutal in man – can with certainty only be maintained to the advantage of the former by organisation, and we think that Anarchism stands self-condemned as to desirability when once these facts are clearly seen.[1] At the same time, it is only fair to remember that the Anarchist does not see this, to most thinkers, obvious truth. His goal and that of the collectivist is the same substantially. But the collectivist would take the sure historic highway of organisation to that Liberty, Equality, and Fraternity which the Anarchist would seek in vain to reach by the abrupt but suicidal plunge of dissolution. It must not be supposed from what is here said that we favour the bourgeois prejudice is to the ineffectiveness of violent revolutions as such. On the contrary, we recognise the teaching of history that no great change has ever taken place without a convulsion or series of convulsions, and we do not believe that the transformation of material conditions which lies before us will be accomplished without some such struggle. But while a collectivist revolution would be constructive at the same time that it would be de-structive, an anarchist revolution would be merely de-structive.

Of the unscientific Socialist standpoints we have passed in review, the most important, numerically and influentially, (more especially, it has the credit on the continent of being the most advanced revolutionary party), is the Anarchist. The least so, inasmuch as it is confined to this country, and to a small body of priests and a limited section of the English middle-class, is that of the Christian and sentimental Socialists respectively. Our reason for devoting so much space to these latter was the desirability in the only English Socialist Review of exposing any "red-herring " which might retard, however slightly or temporarily, the genuine

Socialist movement now beginning in England. Utopian Socialism used as a convenient "aunt-Sally" by Political Economists, who know all the time it is not genuine Socialism they are expounding or attacking, is certainly an irritating, but scarcely a dangerous phenomenon from a practical point of view; while Anarchism does not as yet at least count a "party," however small, in this country. There is probably more danger in Great Britain in a Conservative "red-herring" than in a (so-called) "advanced" one such as Anarchism. With Mr. Henry George we have not dealt, inasmuch as land nationalisation is the child of true Socialism, though it has been by Mr. George "untimely ripped from its mother's womb." Land communisation can only come effectually as the natural issue of a general Socialist revolution. When torn from this connection it can but be abortive.

E. Belfort Bax

## Notes

1. It should be stated that the above criticism applies only in a modified degree, to the (so-called) Communist-Anarchist section of the party.

# The Criminal Court Judge
# (January 1886)

This occupant of the judicial bench is, as we all know, the functionary, selected by the Governmental "ring," to enforce or put into action the cumbrous machinery of law which the civilised world has been compelled to invent as a feeble corrective to the results of its civilisation. We have spoken of the governmental "ring," but might more accurately describe a modern State bureaucracy as a system of "rings" interlacing one within the other. Each "department" has its traditions carefully kept up by its staff of permanent officialdom. The "bosses" of these departments, that is of the central or ministerial ring (and for that matter the others also) emanate, of course, from "Society" as it is termed, that is, from the aristocratic and plutocratic cliques of the West End; but what is more, under our system of party government a particular ministerial post is generally the exclusive appanage of two or three individuals who take it in turns and then begin again. Now the appointment and regulation of the judicial bench rests respectively with the Lord Chancellor and the Home Secretary. It is true the powers of these worthies are practically limited by the "traditions" of the subordinate judicial "ring" itself (a brotherhood as jealous of its privileges and dignity as the Corporation of London or any other mutual benefit society, but appointments, revision of sentences, and general supervision rest it the last resort with the dignitaries in question. The Lord Chancellor, for the most part, appoints the judge from a successful barrister with "influential" connections

Now, our object in thus exposing in a few words the mechanism of our constitutional government in general, and its relation to the judicial system in particular, is the better to grasp the nature of the semi-divinity which with the public at large seems to hedge a judge and all his utterances. The juryman obediently follows his directions as to the verdict it shall return, in fact, in many instance juries would seem to regard it as the sole reason of their being, to please the presiding judge and give glory to him. The public in court, and the public out of court, hang upon the pronouncement from the bench as placing beyond question the enormity of the guilt of the luckless victim (it may be) of judicial rancour. How is this reverence for the judicial fiat to be accounted for? Doubtless, to a large extent, it has its origin like the divine right of kings and many other things in a state of society where the judicial authority was also the religious and civil head of the community in short, that it is one of those numerous sentiments which had a meaning once, in bygone stages of Human Society and intelligence – but which have survived their meaning and hence become superstitions. It is, in fact, only one instance of that respect for law and order in the average mind on which the stability of the Bourgeois state rests, and which masks the true character of the latter as the prop of economical rottenness.

But let us consider for a moment what judgeship involves: We have every day illustrations of the fact that the judicial "ring" presumes upon the respect accorded it, so there can be no doubt that if the people could be induced to see the judge in the light merely of an overpaid servant of the modern state, who absorbs an enormous proportion of their earnings, the better would it be for the soul's welfare of the judicial bench itself, as well as for the cause of the Revolution. Paradox as it may seem it is an undoubted truth that no judge can be an honest man. The judge must necessarily be a man of inferior moral calibre. Though it is a thing I would say, of no other man or body of men, yet I say unhesitatingly that a judge by the fact of his being a judge proclaims himself a creature on a lower moral level than myself – the declaration involving no assumption of moral superiority

87

above the average on my part. And why? Because the aspiring member of the bar when he accepts a judgeship knows that in so doing he deliberately pledges himself to functions which may at any moment compel him to act against his conscience and wrong another man. He deliberately pledges himself, that is, to be false to himself. He may any day have to pass sentence on one whom he believes to be innocent. He lays himself under the obligation of administering a law which he may know to be bad on any occasion when called upon. He makes this surrender of humanity and honour for what? For filthy lucre and tawdry notoriety. Now, I ask, can we conceive a more abjectly contemptible character than that which acts thus? If we want further proof of the utter degeneracy of moral tissue in such a being, let us examine the sophistries he uses in his defence, and which he endeavors on occasion to force down the throat of the recalcitrant juryman. He does not make the law he will tell you, he merely administers it. In the same way Bill Sykes does not make his jemmy and other burglarious implements, he merely administers them. This is the sort of oil he pours on his uneasy conscience when he has one. The juryman disapproving of capital punishment objects to convicting a murderer. He is told he has nothing to do with the sentence, but only with the evidence, in other words that the fact that the verdict he gives will have for its direct consequence a result he regards with abhorrence, is to count for nothing with him. Those who can willingly pretend – I say pretend, since it must be remembered we are dealing with men of ability and culture, capable of exposing many a subtler fallacy when it suits them – men who can pretend to accept such flimsy trash as cogent argument must surely be dead to all respect for honesty and truth.

But the festering mass of hypocrisy of which benchdom consists is only too evident at every turn. There is, of course, the hypocrisy which is racy of the judicial calling just as there is the hypocrisy which is racy of the clerical calling. To this belongs the professed deep reverence for the "law of England," when no one knows better than the benchman who has studied it, that well-nigh one half of English law is based on effete superstition, of which it presents in many cases the most grotesque instances – interesting and instructive from a historical point of view, doubtless, but not in themselves calculated to awaken feelings of reverence in the modern mind – and that the other half is founded on the baldest class interest and prejudice. So that all things considered there is hardly a branch of learning the pursuit of which is more calculated to inspire the average student with a contempt for its subject matter than English Law – hardly even excepting Divinity. But what is more offensive than this is the impudent assumption of moral superiority, which is one of the properties of the profession. Quite apart from any of the considerations just adduced it is perfectly well known that there are among members of the English Bench men of a deb—, well, men that enjoy life on its animal side, as is indeed, only natural considering the amount of time and money on their hands. Yet who can orate with a richer profusion of impressively delivered platitudes of the current morality than the puisne in addressing the prisoner, who has, in ninety nine cases out of a hundred, brought himself within reach of the law by the desire to obtain some of those very pleasures in which the judge himself revels. Now it is scarcely to be expected, but that man who in a "higher" grade of society so called, is capable of accepting a judgeship (with its conditions as described above), would not in a "lower," where the temptations were of a different order and much more severe, be capable of doing a little housebreaking, forgery, or even bigamy or rape. Such being the case the elimination from judicial proceedings of the "John Jacob Jackson you have been convicted on the clearest evidence of etc: To remonstrate with such a man as you would be useless etc., etc.," with the epilogue, "I should be failing in my duty if I did not pass a heavy sentence," etc the elimination I should say, this somewhat stale "gag "from judicial proceedings, might possibly have a tendency to keep alive respect for law somewhat longer than bids fair

89

otherwise to be the case

In France even middle class public opinion has had to assent to the abolition of the scandal of the judge's summing up, but respect for law and order is too great in this country to allow of this instalment of justice towards accused persons. But, surely, even in this country, a muzzle might be applied to the judge after the verdict. If Parliament were to employ itself in doing this it would at least prevent unoffending persons being sickened by the nauseous rant which on the occasion of every important trial now emanates from the whited sepulchre in wig and gown, whose function it is to administer the law.

That society which is based on property and privilege must have a criminal code as its necessary consequence we are well aware but we none the less protest against its "administrator" the judge being regarded in any more honourable light than its other "administrator", the hangman.

E. Belfort Bax

# Some Bourgeois Idols; Or Ideals, Reals, and Shams
## (April 1886)

There are certain catchwords which have a marvellous charm to calm the breast political, a magic power to levitate the mind captivated by them, out of the regions of mere argument and recognition of facts. Such a hold do these words and the deified abstractions they cover have on the average man of the nineteenth century, that they and they alone are worshipped as the ultimate manifestation of goodness, beauty, and truth. To be opposed to these abstractions is to be condemned as blasphemous against the first principles of rectitude, moral and political.

Let us take Liberty. What a charming phrase that is, what a word to conjure with! What a thrill can be evoked from an average audience by the tub-thumper who waves his hand and pronounces the magic formula "liberty of conscience" or "liberty of contract." Little recks the applauding bourgeois whether he has the living reality itself, or merely the empty hull from which the soul has long since fled. Little recks he whether the thing he clasps be human or not. Liberty as expressed in Liberty of contract, of conscience, etc., as understood by the bourgeois of to-day, has been dead well-nigh this three centuries and buried since the French Revolution; the shibboleth that now stalks in its semblance is its vampire, and, like other vampires, if has but one function, to suck the life-blood from its living kin – real liberty.

Time was when our modern "liberty of contract." was the expression of a living reality. Feudal oppression said in effect to the labourer, "You shall only work for one master, for him who is your lord, under whom you were born: you shall work for him for ever, even though he be unjust, harsh, or cruel, and you shall render him his accustomed dues whatever they may be." As against this principle of traditional status the rising bourgeois world invoked "liberty of contract." "Liberty of contract" was then a reality as against its negation, the tyranny of status. The victory of contract over status having been once definitively assured, one might have imagined that liberty was thereby assured also. And this is what the bourgeois, thought and thinks still. He will not recognise the subtle change that has come over "liberty of contract" in the moment of its supremacy – that the tyranny to which it opposed itself is now absorbed into itself. So long as the barren form is there, it matters not to him that by means of the modern revolution in the conditions of production and distribution, its content, its living principle is no longer what it was, but the opposite of what it was – that the body of liberty is animated by the soul of slavery. If once the horror of the ordinary Radical at the sacrilegious hand that would boldly transfix the vampire-body, notwithstanding the honoured shape it bears. He feels the blow struck at liberty of contract is a blow struck at himself, at the core of his being. And in this he is surely not unreasonable. For is he not himself the embodiment of a contract-system? What bourgeois sentiment really cares for and has cared for, in its revolt against status, is not liberty, but the development of the bourgeois world. "Liberty of contract" was essential to this development in its war with status and therefore received honour at its hands, not because of liberty, but because of contract – the power of contract being its only means of realisation. Liberty is the bait held out to the proletarian fish covering the hook of contract. Unless labour can be contracted for, i.e., caught by the capitalist, it is of no more use to them than the fish that remain in the sea are to the fisherman. "Liberty" in the sense of the orthodox economist, is, then, in brief, an empty abstraction which stands in flagrant antagonism to the real, the concrete liberty of the Socialist. The abstract liberty of the economist is the liberty to

92

die quickly of starvation or slowly of the same. The Socialist knows no such liberty as this. He cares not for the liberty to change masters with identical conditions in either case; he cares not for the liberty to refuse work and starve quickly or accept it and starve slowly. He would be glad to see such liberty for ever abolished. The liberty he values is the concrete liberty for individuality to assert itself, the leisure or freedom from work and care which is essential thereto, and which, with comfortable circumstances and good surroundings, make up the sine qua non of all real liberty. Thus the "liberty" which to the mind of the latter Middle Ages was an ideal, and which became a real in the earlier phases of the modern world, has evaporated to a sham in the world of to-day.

"Liberty of conscience" is, again, another of the glib phrases so neatly rolled off the tongue, and which are supposed to crush an opponent against whom they are invoked by their mere intrinsic weight. This, too, as employed by the ordinary Freethinker and Radical, is often but a vampire, a semblance of a reality which has ceased to be. The typical British "Freethinker" would regard with horror as a violation of that sacred idol "liberty of conscience," any attempt under any circumstances to prevent the infusion into mind, incapable of judgment of doctrines which he would admit to be injurious morally and perhaps even physically. His sheet-anchor is argument and reasonable persuasion. But let us take a case. A child or person intellectually incapable either naturally or through ignorance or both, comes under the influence of the Salvation Army or the worst kind of Catholic priest, it matters not which, is terrified by threats of the wrath of God into "conversion," becomes the slave of General Booth or the "Church," is warped morally and mentally for life, and in the worst case possibly driven to religious mania. There's the result of liberty of conscience! The bourgeois Freethinker, hide-bound in this abstraction, is quite oblivious of the fact that, though the form of liberty is there, it does but enshrine the reality of slavery; that it is a liberty to deprive others of liberty. It would be intolerance, forsooth, to suppress the Salvation Army, he will tell you – liberty of conscience demands that the Salvation Army and every other body or individual shall have the privilege of enslaving the mind, of the young or the ignorant by threats or cajolery, of fooling them to the top of their bent. Against this the only weapon he permits himself is argument or persuasion. He forgets that argument is only a reliable weapon when employed against argument, i.e., against a doctrine avowedly based on reason, and that against one which makes its appeal, not to reason, but to faith, fear, and ignorance, argumentative persuasion must be a broken reed. The freedom to hold and propound any proposition, however absurd, as a theory to be judged of, and accepted or rejected at the bar of Reason, is quite another thing from the liberty of the "hot gospeller," who claims to hold a speculative pistol to the ear of ignorant and weak-minded people by threatening them with damnation if they reject his teaching. The one is of the essence of real liberty, the other is the vampire of a dead liberty of conscience which was only living and real when it was opposed to the positive power of the representatives of dogma over men's persons and lives. As Gabriel Deville well puts it, "The aim of collectivity is to assure liberty to each, understanding by this the means of self-development and action, since there can be no liberty where there is the material or moral incapacity of consciously exercising the faculty of will ... To permit by religious practices the cerebral deformation of children is in reality a monstrous violation of liberty of conscience, which can only become effective after the proscription of what at present passes muster for religious liberty, the odious licence in favour of some to the detriment of all." The vampire, bourgeois liberty of conscience, must in short be impaled, before true liberty of conscience can become a healthy living reality.

Let us take another idol. This time we tread on sacred

ground indeed – equality between the sexes. Well may the iconoclastic hand tremble before levelling a blow at this new Serapis. Nevertheless here also – as the phrase is understood by the ordinary modern woman's right, advocate – we are bound to recognise a vampire. In earlier stages of social development, woman was placed in a condition of undoubted social inferiority to man. Into the grounds of this inferiority it is unnecessary here to enter. Suffice it to say it existed, and that against the state of things it implied the cry of "equality between the sexes" was raised, at first in a veiled, and afterwards in an open manner. For some time it represented a real tendency towards equality by the removal of certain undoubted grievances. But for some time past the tendency of the bourgeois world, as expressed in its legislation and sentiment, has been towards a factitious exaltation of the woman at the expense of the man – in other words, the cry for "equality between the sexes" has in the course of its realisation become a sham, masking a de facto inequality. The inequality in question presses as usual, heaviest on working-man, whose wife, to all intents and purposes has him completely in her power. If dissolute or drunken, she can sell up his goods or break up his home at pleasure, and still compel him to keep her and live with her to her life's end. There is no law to protect him. On the other hand, let him but raise a finger in a moment of exasperation against this precious representative of the sacred principle of "womanhood," and straightway he is consigned to the treadmill for his six months amid the jubilation of the D.T. and its kindred, who pronounce him a brute and sing paeans over the power of the "law" to protect the innocent and helpless female. Thus does bourgeois society offer sacrifice to the idol "equality between the sexes." For the law jealously guards, the earnings or property of the wife from possible spoliation. She on any colourable pretext can obtain magisterial separation and "protection."

Again, we have the same principle illustrated in the truly bestial outcry raised every now and again by certain persons for the infliction of the punishment of flogging on men, for particular offences, notably "assaults on women and children." As a matter of fact, in the worst cases of cruelty to children, women are the criminals. Some few months back there was a horrible instance in which a little girl was done to death by a stepmother in circumstances of the most loathsome barbarity: yet these horror-stricken advocates of the lash never venture to support flogging as a wholesome corrective to viragos of this description. It would be opposed to middle-class sentiment, which would regard such a proposition as blasphemy against the sacred principle of "femality." No other explanation is possible, since it can hardly be assumed that even the bourgeois mind is incapable of grasping the obvious fact that a man pinioned and in the hands of half a dozen prison-warders, is in precisely as helpless a condition as any woman in a like cage, and that, therefore, the brutality or cowardice of the proceeding is no greater in the one case than in the other. The bourgeois conception of "equality between the sexes" is aptly embodied in that infamous clause of the "Criminal Law Amendment Act," which provides that in case of illicit intercourse, between a boy and girl under sixteen years of age, though the girl escapes scot free, the boy is liable, to five years imprisonment in a reformatory.

Even the great Radical nostrum which is supposed to involve the quintessence of political equality, is, when closely viewed, the hollowest of shams. The revolutionary socialist perhaps does not much concern himself about questions of the suffrage, esteeming but lightly the privilege of electing men to help to carry on the present system of society, which he believes destined to perish before long. But looked at from the ordinary point of view, it is quite clear that considering the fact that the female population of England is in excess of the male by about a million, female suffrage, in spite of its apparent embodiment of the principle of equality, really means, if it means anything at all (which may be doubtful) the handing over of the complete

96

control of the state to one sex. These are only a few of the illustrations which might be multiplied almost indefinitely, of the truth that the tendency of the modern middle-class world, is, while proclaiming the principle of "equality between the sexes" in opposition to the feudal subjection of woman, to erect, the female sex into a quasi-privileged class. The real equality between the sexes aimed at by socialism is as, I take it, much opposed to this Brummagem sentiment and sham equality, as it is to the female slavery of ancient times of which, of course, we do not wish to deny that survivals remain even at the present day. With the economic emancipation of woman and the gradual transformation of the state-system of to-day into an international league free communes, the feudal subjection of women to man and the middle-class subjection of man to woman will be alike at an end.

Yet another bourgeois idol – the rights of majorities. The Radical mind, instead of placing before it the concrete ideal – Human Happiness, – erects an abstract idol in its room as the supreme end of all endeavour. The Radical's first question is not, does such or such a course conflict with social well-being, but does it not violate one of our supreme dogmas? There is no more frequent charge brought against the revolutionary Socialist than that of despotic interference with the right of the majority. Socialism, it is indeed true, in pursuit of its central purpose, treats with scant reverence the household gods of the Radical. The abstract principle of the right of the majority is of as small concern to the Socialist as the equally abstract principle of "liberty of contract" or " liberty of conscience." And why? Because, like the rest, the bourgeois "right of the majority" is the vampire of a dead reality. Feudalism, and the centralising monarchical tendency which succeeded feudalism proper, opposed the will of the feudal few or of the monarchies) one to the will of the majority of propertied persons, – i.e., the ruling middle class. The ascendancy of this rising middle class then represented the extent of popular aspiration. The decaying principle was Feudalism and the monarchical Absolutism it left behind it. As against the privilege and traditional status upon which this based itself, Liberalism asserted as its ideal the right of the majority of the people as then understood – i.e., of the middle classes – to self-government. Hard upon the realisation of this ideal has followed its reduction to sham. Conditions are changed in the Western Europe of to-day. With the entrance upon the arena of the modern proletariat of capitalism and the differentiation of class interests therein involved, the old popular sovereignty has become a meaningless phrase. The old majority has ceased to be the majority, – has become a minority, and the new majority is in the thraldom of this minority (the franchise notwithstanding). Capitalist fraud has succeeded to feudal force: the castle has given place to the factory.

The new majority, consisting of the proletariat and all those who suffer from the present system, are in the thrall of Capitalism. With no leisure for thought or education, they are necessarily the victims of every sophism of middle-class economists and politicians, even where they are not directly coerced or cajoled by their masters. The majority know that they suffer, they know that they want not to suffer, but they know not why they suffer, and they know not how they may cease to suffer. The majority, therefore, under a capitalist system will necessarily for the most part vote for the maintenance of that system under one guise or another, not because they love it, but out of sheer ignorance and stupidity. It is by the active minority from out the stagnant inert mass that the revolution will be accomplished. It is to this Socialist minority that individuals, acting during the revolutionary period, are alone accountable. The Socialist, leader or delegate, as such, does not take account of the absolute majority of the population, which consists of two sections – i.e., of those who are interested in the maintenance of the present system and those who are blind or inert enough to be misled by them. To disregard the opinion (if such it, can be called) of these latter is no more tyranny than it is tyranny to hold a drunken man back by force when he seeks to get out of the door of a railway carriage with the train going at full speed. The man does not want to be maimed or killed: he is simply misled by his drunken fancy as to what is conducive to his welfare. In the same way the workman who sides with one or other of the various political parties against Socialism, does not want to be the slave of capital, never certain of his next week's lodging and food. In coercing him, if necessary, that is, in negativing his apparent aims, you are affirming his real aims, which are, if nothing more, of least to live in comfort and sufficiency. Yet to grant him the semblance of right, the right to perpetuate his own misery through blindness and to deny him the reality of right by keeping him a slave – the slave of free contract – this is the object of the Liberal and Radical, – an object he hopes to accomplish by, among other things, flaunting in his face the nostrum of the inalienable "rights" of numerical majorities to control of the executive machinery of the state, at all times and in all circumstances. Of course, as soon as Socialism becomes an accomplished fact, the inert mass of indifferentism which now clings to the status quo, not from real class interest, but merely through ignorance and laziness, will be dissolved, and its elements pass over to the new status quo of Socialism. The Socialist party will then cease to exist as a party, and become transformed into the absolute majority of the population. Then, and then only, will the right of the majority and the sovereignty of the people be transformed from a sham into a reality – a fuller reality than it ever has been yet.

A few words on one more "idol," to wit on "justice," as embodied in the "rights of property." It is unjust the Bourgeois will tell you, to nationalise or communise the property now in the hands of private persons, since they as individuals have received it in the natural course of things as guaranteed by social conditions present and past. This notion of the right of every man to the exclusive possession of wealth he has acquired without breach of the criminal law, and of the injustice of depriving him of it, is part and parcel of the system of vampire-dogmas and nostrums of which Liberalism and Radicalism are composed. It has been, like the rest, the ideal principle of the middle-class world in its conflict with Feudalism. In the days of the " small industry," the artificer and the merchant asserted this principle in opposition to the feudal lord. The middle-class world affirmed the absolute right of the individual over all his belongings as against the claims of the overlord and his prescriptive dues, as against tenure in fee generally, and above all as against the dearest right of the mediaeval baron, the right of plunder and dispossession by force of arms. Security of personal property has ever been the middle-class watchword. Hence this new notion of justice.

In the ancient world it would have been deemed "unjust" for the "tribe," the "people," or the "city" to suffer, so long as an individual citizen possessed ought that could relieve that suffering. In the medieval world it would have been "unjust" for the inferior to retain ought that his feudal superior required: while in same cases it would have been "unjust" for the rich man to refuse to give alms to the needy. It would have been "unjust" in the medieval guildsman to have used material of an inferior quality in his work or to have employed more apprentices and journeymen than the rules of his guild permitted. But as we have said, to the corruption and rapacity which characterised the decaying feudal classes at the break up of the mediaeval system, the bourgeois opposed his thesis of the inviolability of private property and of the ideal of justice consisting in the absolute control of his property by the individual. But, like the rest, this principle unimpeachable as it seemed, had no sooner realised itself, than its reality began to wane. Now, in this last quarter of the nineteenth century it is dead, and stalks the world as perhaps the ghastliest "vampire" of all. The immediate cause of its transition from the living to the lifeless is the change from small individual production to co-operative production, – a change which has reached its consummation in the "great industry." Yet strange to say, the Liberal or Radical can still mouth about the injustice of expropriating the wealthy few for the good of the whole. To him there is no "injustice" in the chronic starvation of myriads of his fellow-men, in the robbery of their labour and health and lives by the rich man by means of his wealth: yet there is "injustice" in depriving the Vanderbilt of a single hundred or the Duke of Argyll of a single acre!

But it is time to drop the curtain on the grim procession. Veritably this last of the bloodless spectres – bourgeois "Justice" – will not bear looking on. It is death on the pale horse habited in nineteenth century humbug. The hope and aim of the Socialist must be to lay these troubled ghosts – to consign them to their lower resting-place. Then will "liberty," "equality," "right," and "justice" once more flourish living and real, not in their old forms indeed, which are henceforth for ever dead and meaningless, but in higher and nobler ones. The evolution which we have: traced in them through their seeming negation to a higher reality is but one instance of the inherent dialectic of the world, in which death and destruction evince themselves the inseparable conditions of life and progress.

E. Belfort Bax

# Imperialism v. Socialism
# (February 1885)

We seem at, the present time to have arrived at the acute stage of the colonial fever which during the last three or four years has afflicted the various powers of Europe. Germany is vying with France, England with both, in the haste to seize upon "unoccupied" countries, and to establish "protectorates" – the cant diplomatic for incomplete annexation – over uncivilised peoples. "The rivalry among the nations for their share of the world market" (to quote the words of our manifesto) must now, one would think, have discovered itself to even the casual newspaper reader as the only meaning the terms "diplomacy" and "foreign policy" any longer possess. The jealousy between the courts of Europe, once the sole and until recently the main cause of national enmity and war, has in our day been superseded by the jealousy between the great capitalists of its various nationalities. The flunkey-patriot, zealous of his country's honour, dances as readily to-day to the pipe of capitalist greed as he did before to that of royal intrigue, let it but sound the note of race-hatred. In both cases he makes the running for the interested parties. But where the interested party is the wealthiest and most powerful class, able to pay for "patriotic" articles by the yard, and "patriotic" speeches by the hour, "patriotism" is apt to assume the form of a chronic disease. Such it is, to-day, and, as such mocks the futile efforts of the well-meaning but singularly ingenuous clique of middle-class philanthropists, who are naive enough to take the governmental ring at its word when it pretends its only object in undertaking "expeditions" to be the rescue of "Christian heroes" or the relief of garrisons which have no right to be in a position to want relieving. War, jingoism – otherwise patriotism – are indeed past cure while the economic basis of society remains unchallenged, but only so far; and hence we call on all sincere friends of peace to leave their tinkering "peace societies" and work for Socialism, remembering that all commercial wars – and what modern wars are not directly or indirectly commercial? – are the necessary outcome of the dominant civilisation. We conjure them to reflect that such wars must necessarily increase in proportion to the concentration of capital in private hands – i.e., in proportion as the commercial activity of the world is intensified, and the need for markets becomes more pressing. Markets, markets, markets! Who shall deny that this is the drone-bass ever welling up from beneath the shrill howling of "pioneers of civilisation", "avengers of national honour," "purveyors of gospel light," "restorers of order;" in short, beneath the hundred and one cuckoo cries with which the "market classes" seek to smother it or to vary its monotony? It seems well-nigh impossible there can be men so blind as not to see through these sickening hypocrisies of the governing classes, so thin as they are.

But we would above all earnestly urge the workers in future to consider "patriotism" from this point of view. The end of all foreign policy, as of colonial extension, is to provide fields for the relief of native surplus capital and merchandise, and to keep out the foreigner. But how, we ask, does this benefit the workers at the best? They are allowed, may be, the privilege of being shipped across the seas, there to help to make the colonialist and land-grabber rich. Some few here and there, may, indeed, succeed in a colony which is quite new, in becoming wealthy exploiters in their turn. But the immense majority remain wage-slaves as before. In proportion to the advancing prosperity of the colony – as prosperity is conceived in the world of to-day – is its advancing poverty. Sydney, Melbourne, San Francisco, Chicago, and the leading Australian and New American cities generally, exhibit precisely the same conditions as the cities of the Old World. And how should it be otherwise, since the same causes are at work? To crown dependencies like India, which are

103

held unblushingly as magazines for the aristocratic and middle classes to plunder at their will, it is only necessary to barely allude in a socialist journal.

This, then, is the empire which the blood and sinew of you, workers, are squandered to maintain and extend. With room enough and to spare in the British Islands for all their inhabitants to live a comfortable life, ever fresh lands are sought for exploitation, ever new populations for pillage. It matters not even that colonies already established could accommodate more than a hundred times their present inhabitants; still the vampire Imperialism sucks in fresh territory year by year. Populations to rob and enslave; markets to shoot bad wares into; lands to invest capital upon: to obtain these is the be-all and end-all of modern statesmanship. For this has the stock jobbers' republic of France waged war successively on Tunis, Madagascar, Tonquin, and China; for this does the thieves' congress sit at Berlin, partitioning the plunder of Central Africa in advance; for this does Bismarck seize Angra Pequena, New Ireland, and Samoa; for this the sham fanatic and heroic restorer of corrupt Chinese despotism reluctantly (?) consents to go to Khartoum on a pacific mission, collects a body of adventurers on his arrival, proceeds to attack the surrounding tribes, and then shrieks for British troops to protect him; for this, lastly, is Lord Wolseley sent with an expedition in response, up the Nile.[1]

And now a word as to the attitude of Socialists towards the imperial question. For the Socialist the word frontier does not exist; for him love of country, as such, is no nobler sentiment than love of class. The blustering "patriot," big with England's glory, is precisely on a level with the bloated plutocrat, proud to belong to that great "middle class," which he assures you is the "backbone of the nation." Race-pride and class-pride are, from the standpoint of Socialism, involved in the same condemnation.

The establishment of Socialism, therefore, on any national or race basis is out of the question.

No, the foreign policy of the great international Socialist party must be to break up these hideous race monopolies called empires, beginning in each case at home. Hence everything which makes for the disruption and disintegration of the empire to which he belongs must be welcomed by the Socialist as an ally. It is his duty to urge on any movement tending in any way to dislocate the commercial relations of the world, knowing that every shock the modern complex commercial system suffers weakens it and brings its destruction nearer. This is the negative side of the foreign policy of Socialism. The positive is embraced in a single sentence: to consolidate the union of the several national sections on the basis of firm and equal friendship, steadfast adherence to definite principle, and determination to present a solid front to the enemy.

## Notes

1. Since the above was written, the Nile expedition has failed, and the Soudan been abandoned. The capitalist found that Khartoum, as a market for white "duck" trousers and Brummagem gewgaws, world not pay for the expenses of keeping, at all events at present. Burmah was found to be a more profitable field for the policy of the capitalist. In consequence King Theebaw became very wicked.

# The Two Enthusiasms
# An Answer to Mr. Karl Pearson
# (February 1886)

IN a pamphlet recently issued[1], Mr. Karl Pearson has undertaken to assault the fortress of Revolutionary Socialism from the academic side. We are commonly enough bombarded by the professional economist, by the theologian, by the politician, by the "sentimentalist," but the man of culture" has hitherto confined himself to the drizzling infantry fire of casual criticism. In Mr. Pearson, however, we are bound to recognise an opponent not to be despised, and in his pamphlet a well-planned attack. To drop metaphor, Mr. Pearson, whether he intended it or not, has stated a specious case for the nice young man fresh from the university, who shudders at the "coarseness" inseparable from a real working-class movement, and prefers the attitude of missionary of culture to the benighted proletarian heathen to that of his co-worker in the cause of social emancipation and in the hurrying on of that class-struggle which is its necessary condition. His argument may also to some extent be considered an elaborate justification of another individual, namely of him who really feels that he is essentially unfit for the work of agitation, and that his most useful sphere is in purely intellectual labour, which may quite possibly be Mr. Pearson's own case. We may say at once that so far as we can see, the last-named individual requires no justification at all, since Socialists should be the first, to recognise diversity of capacity – diversity albeit largely intensified by current conditions – and that the "nice young man" deserves none, save that like the "coarse" proletarian to whom he condescends to direct his missionary efforts, he may plead that he is but the unfortunate result of a vicious system.

106

With the opening paragraphs of the pamphlet in question which deal with the distinction between natural and supernatural morality, I heartily agree. Strange to say, on page 3 Mr. Pearson argues for a kind of neo-Puritanism; he would apparently give an introspective turn to social ethics, whereby the attention would still be directed primarily to the formation of individual character, rather than to the clear and broad issues of social life and progress. We may have mistaken the author's meaning, but we must confess the prospect strikes us as rather appalling if the "trivial doings" of each day (let us say, for instance, taking a walk round the room) are previously to performance, to pass the scrutiny of an internal examination as to whether they or the motives prompting them, are "dictated by those general laws, which have been deduced," etc. Certain broad lines of conduct clearly hostile to 'the existence of social life are to be shunned, other broad lines are to be followed – what more does an ethic founded on social necessity mean than this? Surely, the hair-splitting casuistry of a theological morality, based upon the notion that every action has an "absolute value," and is certain to be rigidly assayed by a heavenly pawnbroker, is out of place here. The resuscitation, too, of that ancient fallacy, that the test of the value or the truth of a doctrine is to be found, not in itself, but in its advocate, I must confess surprises me in a man of Mr. Pearson's ability. His remarks on this head recall to my mind the would-be crushing argument of the Christian advocate of a generation ago, that Voltaire was a "bad man," and that hence his attack on Christianity is discredited at the outset. Also, that the authors of the Gospels were good men, and, therefore, they were to be believed. Hegel, we are quite aware, was by no means a man of heroic moral calibre, but this does not prevent his reading of the riddle of Life and Knowledge being, not even excepting Spinoza's, take it all in all, the least unsatisfactory up to date. As a matter of fact, as history proves over and over again, there is seldom an equal balance between the intellectual and moral sides of a gifted man's character, so that in general we should naturally expect a man of exceptional power in the one direction to be deficient in the other.

Turning to the main theme of the pamphlet under consideration, we find the baneful influence of the individualistic and absolute ethics which the outset of the paper led us to hope Mr. Pearson had outgrown again at work. To the Revolutionary Socialist Mr. Pearson says, "Abandon agitation, go and create a new morality." Now, from the point of view of a Scientific Socialism, he might as well tell the engineer, "Abandon your borings and your blastings, say to yonder mountain, depart thou hence and be thou cast into the sea, for until the ground is level you will never make your highway." Mr. Pearson is evidently still more than half a Christian, leastways in his ethics. He thinks that all social change must proceed from the individual; that all reform must come from within, in accordance with Christian doctrine, but in striking defiance of the teaching of history and what I may term a concrete view of the nature of things. Morality is with Mr. Pearson an abstract entity, to be brought to perfection by a culture of the individual breathed out in some mysterious manner from the study, and operating by a magic charm of its own on squalid masses huddled in reeking courts, on the outcast in the recesses of London Bridge, on the factory slave or the shop-assistant without leisure and resources, on the out-of-work labourer with starvation at his door, no less than on the struggling shopkeeper whose being's end and aim is to hold out against the big capitalist competitor, and last of all on the giant capitalist himself – on the Vanderbilt or the Jay Gould. It is to operate, in short, irrespective of such insignificant obstacles as economic conditions and social surroundings. The factory-slave and the Vanderbilt are alike to feel the renovating influence touch their hearts, to hear the voice of "Culture" and live – a pleasant dream forsooth. Unfortunately, according to Mr. Pearson's own estimate it may take some hundreds of years, and "'while the grass grows –'. The proverb is something musty." Mr. Pearson in his study may be content to wait, but will social evolution wait?

108

"Human society cannot, be changed in a year," says our critic. True, answers the Socialist, but its economic conditions can be radically modified in a very few years through the concentration of the means of production and distribution in the hands of a Socialist administration. Thus although one generation may not indeed suffice to complete the transformation of Civilisation into socialism, yet even one generation may dig the foundation of the fabric, nay, the time being ripe, may even rough-hew its more prominent outlines. We readily admit that the old leaven of civilisation must require many a long decade before it is eliminated, but the generation which for the first time turned the helm of progress in the one direction by which its goal can be reached, would be worthy of none the less honour because it was not itself destined to see the promised land in its fulness. Thenceforward we shall be consciously steering for the goal towards which hitherto we have been at best only unconsciously and vaguely drifting; the whole political and administrative system, when once the great crisis of the revolution is passed, instead of, as now, having for its sole aim the perpetuation of itself and of the class antagonisms it represents, will have for its end the abolition of civilisation, that is, of a class-society, and therewith its own abolition, since with the transformation of Civilisation into socialism it will be a superfluous and meaningless survival.

In the pamphlet before us we have once more the hackneyed argument that the French Revolution left no enduring creation behind it, that it was abortive in short. Has Mr. Pearson ever read Arthur Young? Has be forgotten the state of France, before and after the Revolution? Nay, not of France only, but of entire western Europe? What was there of human creation in the French Revolution? asks Mr. Pearson. There was the creation, at all events, of the supremacy of the commercial middle class (though there is not much that is "human" in that, I admit). The French Revolution meant the final realisation of Bourgeoisdom, –

109

this was its central idea and purpose, – notwithstanding that it contained episodes which pointed to something beyond this. Into Mr. Pearson's special preserve of the Reformation I will not enter particularly, except to say that as I read history a similar observation holds good there also.

The "enthusiasm of the study" is by no means a new thing. It is as old at least as Periklean Greece. In the "garden," the "grove," and the "porch," we have the enthusiasts of the study; and in the later grammarians enthusiasts who despised the "marketplace" possibly even more than Mr. Pearson himself. Yet, cannot we date the decline of ancient culture precisely from the moment when it became the exclusive appanage of the study? This high-toned ancient enthusiasm of the study, did it make a good end? Or did it not rather ignominiously "peter out" in the persons of the seven melancholy and neglected sages or pedants, who wandered in dry places seeking rest and finding none till the worthy Chosroes obtained them a respite for the term of their natural lives wherein to reflect, on the vanity of that empyrean "enthusiasm of the study" which had become so rarefied that no mortal besides themselves could breathe its atmosphere? Need I remind Mr. Pearson of other enthusiasms of the study? Setting aside the German humanists, whose work, Mr. Pearson would say, was rendered abortive by the wicked men of the market-place, let us turn to the Italian renaissance, the courts of the Medicis. Here the "enthusiasm of the sturdy" was disturbed by no red-herring of the market-place. Yet what did it effect for mankind at large? What of the French salon-culture of the eighteenth century? For even Mr. Pearson, we suppose, will hardly contend that had it not been for the market-place Revolution which ensued, the "philosophers" and Litterateurs of the study would have regenerated mankind by the influence of their conversation on the wits, bons vivants, and fascinating women of eighteenth century France. "Sweetness and light," again – the refined, esthetic, middle-class culture of to-day –

what has this gospel of "sweet reasonableness" done, what does it bid fair to do? Brought together interesting young men from the universities to study the habits of the East-end "poor," perhaps; provided a temporary stimulus in the direction of soup-kitchens and "literary institutes." Is Mr. Karl Pearson content with such a result?

But the root-fallacy of Mr. Pearson's pamphlet lies, to our thinking, deeper than this. It lies, namely, in his attempt to accentuate the distinction which civilisation has in great part created between the "study" and "the market-place," the man of learning and the man of labour, and to treat it as permanent. To the Socialist this is merely one of the abstractions produced by a society based on classes and, therefore, is essentially false and unreal, and as such destined to pass away with the other abstractions – e.g. ruler and ruled, master and servant, capital and labour, rich and poor, religious and secular, etc. – which find their expression in modern civilisation. The enthusiasm of the market-place and the enthusiasm of the study are not properly two things, but one. They form part of one whole. The enthusiasm of the market-place is the direct expression of the particular phase at which social evolution has arrived, the enthusiasm of the study is its indirect expression. The present, enthusiasm of the study with the large place modern science occupies in it, differs from the old humanist enthusiasm of the fifteenth century, as that differed from the enthusiasm of the medieval schoolmen, and so on; and we may add it differs from the enthusiasm of the future, when mathematics shall have been relegated to their due place in the economy of human culture. But the enthusiasm of the study per se is no substantial body; though fair in semblance, it is after all but a bloodless wraith. As little can you require the "enthusiasm of the study" to supplant the "enthusiasm of the market-place" in human society, as St. Denis could have expected his decapitated head to urge him on irrespective of the trunk to which it belonged. That the first condition of the healthy animal is a good

111

digestion is a trite observation. The first condition of a healthy society, as certainly, is that it should have something to digest, something besides Pearsonic morality, wholesome as that may be in its proper place. In other words, the intellectual and moral revolution of society rests primarily upon the conditions in which its wealth is produced and distributed. When this is done in the interest of all, and when all take an equal share in it, then that embodied abstraction, the "man of the study," will disappear along with that other embodied abstraction, "the man of the market-place." In a society in which culture is for all, and work is for all, the antagonism of the workman and the scholar will be resolved in the concrete reality of the complete human being. Meanwhile, so long as the antagonism exists, it is plainly the market-place that must create the revolution, since it has the material power in its hands, and this it is which constitutes, the enthusiasm of the of the market-place, unreasoning and "emotional" though it be, the great moving force of society.

E. Belfort Bax

## Notes

1. The Enthusiasm of the Study and of the Market Place, a lecture delivered at South Place Institute, Finsbury, by Karl Pearson.

# The Capitalist Hearth
# (May 1886)

THE throne, the altar, and the hearth – the political emblem, the religious emblem, and the social emblem – have long constituted the mystic trinity to which appeal is made when popular class-sentiment is required to be invoked against influences, disintegrative of the status quo. In the bourgeois world of to-day the first two terms may be sometime modified. The middle-class man's respect for the throne per se may, be more or less diluted; he may even prefer to substitute for it the presidential chair, but in either case it is the "law" – the legal system of a class-society – which is typified; to the altar he might possibly prefer the "Bible," by which he would wish to be understood Protestant dogmas without the inconveniences of direct sacerdotal domination. Such slight modifications of the original formulae as these matter little, however, since in any case the old feudal sentiment for the liege temporal and spiritual has been long since dead. The old formula may, therefore, be conveniently adopted as an indication of the three aspects of the modern world, which its votaries are so jealous of preserving. Beneath throne, altar, and hearth, in their present form, all socialists know that there lies the market. They know that the market is the bed-rock on which the throne, the altar, and the hearth of the nineteenth century rest, and that this bed-rock shattered, the said throne, altar, and hearth will be doomed.

Respecting the throne and the altar we have not much to say in the present article. It is with the bulwark of social life, the hearth, otherwise expressed as modern family-life that we are here chiefly concerned. We refer more especially to the family life whose special architectural expression is the suburban villa.

This is the ideal of the middle-class family of a "lower" i.e., poorer degree, while in those of a "higher," i.e., richer degree, its characteristics are exaggerated into the rank luxuriance symbolised in the brand-new country mansion. Let us consider briefly the characteristics of the suburban villa in its daily life, and surroundings much as we would that of some ancient people, as thus:–

I. Household Ways; early morning (item 1) Prayers. (2) breakfast. (3) Departure of paterfamilias and sons to business, Journey beguiled by morning papers and conversation resembling for the most part undigested "leaders" from same. (N.B. The modern journalist is, as it were, the cook who boils down and seasons up into a presentable entree the "dead cats" of middle-class prejudice.) (4) At home the wife and daughters, after a possible feint at domestic duties, prepare for "shopping." (5) "Shopping," the main occupation in the day for the woman of the middle class being over, luncheon follows, then calls, then afternoon tea. (6) Return of paterfamilias, more or less worried with his daily round of laboriously endeavouring to shift money from his neighbour's pocket into his own, wearied, i.e., and degraded, with doing no useful work whatever. (7) Evening taken up with sleep, or conversation on the affairs of the family; together with its relations and connections, varied with the indifferent performance of fashionable music and the perusal of "current" literature. The above, we contend, is a fair picture of the type toward which the daily life of the average English middle-class family gravitates. We have said English, inasmuch as the commercial system has been more potent in its effect on English domestic life than on that of any other European people; but the same tendency to vapidity, inanity, pseudo-culture, which is the worst form of lack of refinement, obtains to a greater or less extent wherever a commercial middle-class exists. A few words now on the art, the literature, the sentiment, moral and religious, of the class in question.

First, as to the house decoration. Not to speak of furniture proper, what do we see on the walls? Art embodied in "furniture" pictures, among them often times the terrible counterfeit presentment of connections of the family, which, were there a vestige of taste left in the household management, would never be exposed to the gaze even of the casual visitor. The superficiality of average middle-class culture is painfully illustrated in the complete ignorance displayed by the middle-class man or woman as to the ugliness or commonplaceness of his or her relations. We quite admit, that, the ancestors or "connections" of a family, may have a certain historical importance for those interested in its natural history, but, save in a very few cases, the interest attaching to them is limited to this. Now, we contend that this does not justify the obtrusion of what is intrinsically disagreeable. There is undoubtedly considerable historical interest in (say) a well-preserved human abortion, but inasmuch as there is that in it which is intrinsically unpleasant, the savant of sensibility keeps it reserved under lock and key for private contemplation. True culture gives a man the powers of rising above the standpoint of his immediate interests and of taking an objective view of things. It may be too much to expect of a man ever to see himself as others see him, but surely he might see his relations as others see them.

Apart from portraits what other art does our middle-class parlour present? "Reproductions" by processes varying in badness according to the length of the family purse. In some instances these mechanical reproductions may be of the old masters, in which case they are perhaps the best thing procurable in the way of art. But for the artist it is surely a melancholy best when art in the family is represented by such. Again, let us take furniture and household decorations. A visit to any large upholsterer's shop will suffice to show the superficiality of the varnish of "taste" in matters decorative, even where absolute sordidness does not prevail. But the English lower middle-class

115

family parlour, or the never-entered drawing-room of the next grade! Can the "family" which alas produced these things be in any way worth preserving?

If it be thought that its art and furniture are only superficial, local, and temporary accidents of the modern family, it is only necessary to turn to the rest of its products, to be convinced how very consistently everything connected with it hangs together. Its literature may be divided into two classes – the variable and the constant. The first consists in the circulating library three-volume novel, in which one section of middle-class womanhood delights; the second in "books" designed for "family reading." mostly of a moral or religious tendency, got up in bright colours and gilt leaves, and available at every suburban or provincial bookseller's or stationer's shop, in which another section delights. This class of literature, by the production of which many clergymen of insufficient stipend, and spinsters with disordered organic functions, gain a livelihood; was until the last few years the sole kind certain to be available in the typical middle-class "home." Its way of life, it must be admitted, has fallen some what into the sere and yellow leaf of late, but it flourishes more or less still, as the publishing firms of Griffith &- Farran, Nisbet & Co., the Religious Tract Society, and even Cassell, Petter & Galpin, will testify.

Closely connected with this subject is that of religious practices. Religion in one or other of its forms is a staple ingredient of bourgeois family life in this country. It constitutes the chief amusement of the women of the family, who find in Sunday school teaching, district visiting, bazaars, etc., a virtuous mode of relieving themselves of the ennui which otherwise could not fail to overtake their empty lives. The singular part of it is, that with all the attempts of these respectable unfortunates to enlighten and elevate the "poor," there is an entire absence of all suspicion that they themselves need enlightening and elevating. Of late years we note, as a sign of the times, that there has been a tendency to modification of the teaching from theology to economy. Evangelicism with its "conversions," its "changes of heart," has fallen decidedly flat of late, even with that half-educated middle class, which some quarter of a century ago were its most prominent votaries. It is tacitly acknowledged to be out of date. Its catchwords, moreover, now that they have been dragged through the Salvation Army, and had to serve as convenient trade-marks for tea, sugar, and other groceries, and, in fact, make themselves generally useful to the enterprising firm of Booth & Sons, look decidedly the worse for wear. After the appearance in a provincial town (as reported in the newspapers some time ago) of the ingenious advertisement of a Salvation Army meeting, running, "Why give 10d. a pound for mutton when you can get the lamb of God for nothing?" the well-known phrase is perhaps deemed spoiled for the ministrations of the respectable wife or daughter. There is the possible danger of getting mixed-up with the "army" and its proceedings. Be this as it may, the fact remains that "thrift," "teetotalism," "industry," and the rest, of the economic virtues, are superseding "immediate repentance," "coming to the Saviour," etc., as the subjects for exhortation in the visitation of the poor.

But, however unfashionable the old dogmatics may become, there is one institution which will certainly hold its own so long as the bourgeois family lasts, and that is the "place of worship." In contemporary British social life the church or chapel is the rendezvous or general club for both sexes; it is the centre, in many places, round which the melancholy institution of the suburban or provincial evening party circulates. It is the bureau de marriage for the enterprising youth who goes to business to qualify for "success in life," and the commercial virgin anxious to be settled, to meet and form connections. Besides all this, it serves the purpose of a fashionable lounge, where the well-dressed may disport themselves and make physiognomical observations if that way inclined. So, all things considered, the "place of worship" may watch unconcernedly the decay of dogma so long as the "great middle class" maintains its supremacy – in this country at least.

We defy any human being to point to a single reality, good or bad, in the composition of the bourgeois family. It has the merit of being the most perfect specimen of the complete sham that history has presented to the world. There are no holes in the texture through which reality might chance to peer. The bourgeois hearth dreads honesty as its cat dreads cold water. The literary classics that are reprinted for its behoof it demands shall be rigorously Bowdlerised, even though at the expense of their point. Topics of social importance are tabooed from rational discussion, with the inevitable result that erotic instances of middle-class womanhood are glad of the excuse afforded by "good intentions," "honest fanaticism," and the like things supposed to be associated with "Contagious Diseases Act" and "Criminal Law Amendment" agitations, to surfeit themselves on obscenity. And these are the people who cannot allow unexpurgated editions of Boccaccio or even of Sterne or Fielding to be seen on their drawing-room tables! Then again, the attitude of the "family" to the word "damn." Now, if there is a honest straightforward word in the English language – a word which the Briton utters in the fulness of his heart – it is this word; and precisely, as it would seem, for this reason it is a word which is supposed never to enter the "family;" even newspapers, in order to maintain their right of entrance to the domestic sanctuary, having to print it with a "d" and a dash – the meaning of which euphemism, by a polite fiction the "wife" or "daughter" is supposed not to understand But the word is coarse and offensive in itself, the bourgeois may retort. You have tried to make it so, I reply, by classing it with the filthy and inane, phrases, bred of the squalor which modern capitalism creates, but in reality it is good,

118

expressive English. Nay, more, it has "higher claims on your consideration" – to employ one of your own phrases, – it bears the impress of Christianity upon it; for is it not to Christianity that we are indebted for the "spiritual significance" of the word? It was always a puzzle to me why the bare allusion to a Christian institution should be so offensive to the ears of the Christian household. In fact, in common consistency you ought to reduce the "damns" of your New Testaments to "d—s," to make the work suitable for family reading. You do not do this, and why? Because your real objection to the colloquial "damn" is, as already remarked, that it has a ring of honest sentiment in it; against which your sham family sentiment revolts.

Let us take another "fraud" of middle-class family life – the family party. That ever and anon a wide circle of friends should meet together in a spirit of good fellowship is clearly right and rational; but the principle of the family party is that a body of persons often having nothing whatever in common but ties of kinship extending in remoteness from the definiteness of blood relation to the indefiniteness of connection – that such a motley crew – should meet together in exclusive conclave, and spend several mortal hours in simulated interest in each other. Now a cousin, let us say, may be an interesting person ; but very often he is not. If he is not, why should one be expected every 25th of December or other occasion, to make a point of spending one's leisure with a man who is a cousin but not interesting, rather than with another man who is interesting but not a cousin? The reason is, of course, that the tradition of the "family" has to be kept up. A "relation," however remote, is, in the eyes of bourgeois society, more to a man than a friend, however near. So relations, male and female, congregate together on certain occasions to do dreary homage to this "family" sentiment.

On the same principle the symbolical black of mourning

is graduated by the tailor and milliner in mathematically accurate ratio, according to the amount, not of affection, but of relationship. The utter and ghastly rottenness of Bourgeois family sentiment, is in nothing more clearly evinced than in the mockery of grief and empty ostentation of tailoring and millinery displayed on the death of a near relation. What is the first concern of the middle-class household the instant the life-breath has left one of its members but to "see after the mourning," as the expression is? Surely, to a person of sensibility the notion that the moment he enters on his last sleep his or her relations will see about the mourning" may well impart to death a terror which it had not before, and this act as an incentive to carefully-concealed suicide. We believe indeed the frequency of "mysterious disappearances" in middle-class circles maybe largely explained by this, without resorting to far-fetched hypotheses of midnight murders on the Thames embankment, and the like? To signify a bereavement to the outer world (if so desired) by a band of crape on the sleeve or hat, or some such simple emblem, is one thing; to eagerly take advantage of the bereavement for the purpose of decking out the person in trousers designed in the newest cut adapted for the display of the male leg, or "bodies" in which the fulness of the female breast is manifested, is quite another, and nothing less than a ghastly travesty of the sentiment.

This, then, is the "hearth," this the family life, the family sentiment, which certain writers are so jealous of preserving. In vain do enthusiastic young persons band themselves together, under the benediction of the "old man" of Coniston, into societies of St.. George, in the hope that the low level of modern social life, with its vulgarity, its inanity, and its ugliness, by some wondrous educational stimulus, emanating from their own enthusiastic and artistic souls, may undergo a process of upheaval. After some years of Ruskinian preaching, what is the net result? A sprinkling of households among specially literary and artistic circles where better things are attempted, and so far as

120

the elements of furniture and decoration are concerned, perhaps with some measure of success. But even here you commonly find the counterbalancing evil inevitably attending a hothouse culture out of harmony with general social conditions – viz., affectation and self-consciousness. No healthy living art or culture has ever been the result of conscious effort. When it, comes to saving "go to, now, let us be wise," or "let us be artistic," it is quite certain that the wisdom or art resulting will not be worth very much. The distinction between an artificial culture of this sort, which is cut off from the life of the society as a whole, and the natural culture which grows out of such life, is as the difference between a flower plucked from its root arid withering in the hand, and the same flower growing in luxuriance on its native soil. For what, after all, has modern art to offer but at best the plucked flowers of the art of the past, which sprang out of the life of the past? Your societies of St. George, your esthetic movements, etc., only touch a fringe of the well-to-do classes: they have no root in the life of the present day; and because they have no root they wither away, and in a few years remain dried up between the pages of history to mark the place of mistaken enthusiasm and abortive energies. It. is surely tune that these excellent young people, together with their beloved prophet, descended for a while from their mount of Ruskinian transfiguration, with its rolling masses of vaporous sentiment, to the prosaic ground of economic science, and saw things as they are.[1] They would then recognise the vanity of their efforts, and the reason of this vanity to lie in their disregard of the economic foundation and substructure of all human affairs; they would see the radical impossibility of the growth of any real art, culture, or sentiment, in the slimy ooze of greed and profit-mongering – in other words, in a society resting on a capitalistic basis. They would see, further, that the end of the world of profit and privilege cannot be attained by enthusiasms, good intentions, or any available farm of class culture, but will have to be reached by a very different route – maybe through February rioting; and possibly still rougher things.

The transformation of the current family-form, founded as it is on the economic dependence of women, the maintenance of the young and the aged falling on individuals rather than on the community, etc., into a freer, more real and, therefore, a higher form, must, inevitably follow the economic revolution which will place the means of production and distribution under the control of all for the good of all. The bourgeois "hearth, with its jerry-built architecture, its cheap art, its shoddy furniture, its false sentiment, its pretentious pseudo-culture, will then be as dead as Roman Britain.

E. Belfort Bax

## Notes (by William Morris)

1. I think that whatever damage Ruskin may have done to his influence by his strange burst of fantastic perversity, he has shown much insight even into economical matters, and I am sure he has made many Socialists; his feeling against Commercialism is absolutely genuine, and his expression of it most valuable. - W.M.

# Civil Law under Socialism
# Contract and Libel
# (24 July 1886)

IT is a common thing for persons to incorporate with their conceptions of a Socialistic state of society elements drawn from the present one, and then to complain of the incongruity of the result. Few persons dream, for instance, that the present elaborate and complex judicial system, or something like it, will not obtain then as much as now. Hence the "difficulties" of so many worthy people.

"Law" is commonly divided into the familiar categories of civil law and criminal law, though legal pedantry could doubtless confound the distinction. By civil law we understand, in accordance with current usage, law concerned with disputes between individuals involving acts which are non-criminal or of which the criminal law takes no cognisance, including all law relating to contract, or the obtaining of damages for injuries, not punishable as criminal offences. It is this department of law upon which we wish to say a few words.

Now we contend that from the moment the State acquires a definite social end – the moment, that is, the machinery of government is taken possession of by, in the name, and for the sake of, the working classes, with a view to the abolition of classes – the whole department of law will become an anachronism which it will be incumbent upon the executive, whatever form it may take, to immediately sweep away. A very little reflection will suffice to show (as the phrase goes) that the civil law referred to is an entirely class-institution, designed (1) in the interest of that class within a class so powerful throughout all periods of civilisation – viz., the legal class, and (2) of the privileged and possessing classes generally. The first point is a trite observation to every one. We all know that "going to law" profits the lawyers more than the litigants on either side. The second point is scarcely less clear. The wealthy litigant is the only person for whom law is even available, for the most part, and certainly the only person for whom it can ever be profitable. The fear of litigation is a weapon society places in the hands of the rich man to coerce the poor man, irrespective of the merits of the case, by dangling ruin before him. If we examine any ground of civil action, we shall find it almost always turns directly or indirectly on a question of property – that is, on what individual shall possess certain wealth – the chances being invariably on the side of the wealthy litigant.

But it may be said, cannot civil law be divested of its class character, and thus serve an intermediary purpose at least in the initial stage of Socialism, when current conditions are still surviving, by constituting the judge, advocate, etc., a mere public servant or functionary, remunerated no more highly than the scavenger? Could not civil "justice" thus be made readily available for all? Perhaps it might, we reply, but it would be anti-Socialistic all the same. Civil law, like all special products of civilisation, is essentially individualistic. It is concerned with the relations of two propertied individuals, one with the other, and as such cannot concern a society established even incompletely on a Socialistic basis. What recks such a society or its administrators of the private quarrels of individuals? Wilful violence done to any member of society, whatever shape it takes, is a matter which affects society as a whole – an offence against society and hence criminal in kind, whatever its degree. But the more or less obscure question as to who is in the right in a personal quarrel cannot possibly concern society as a whole. Two would-be

124

parties in a civil action, were they to attempt to inflict their squabble upon a community even so much as on the way towards being socialised would surely deserve to be treated in the spirit in which the housewife possessed of a slop-pail is wont to treat two domestic cats that plead their causes plaintively upon the roofs at midnight. At present, of course, in a state busied in individual exploitation and scramble for possession, it matters not that an elaborate machinery is maintained, involving numbers of persons being kept from productive labour – in other words involving a waste of social power – for the sake of deciding quarrels; indeed, this machinery is an essential element in such a systems of society. For is not, the economic corner-stone of this society, contract, and do not the bulk of civil actions hinge on questions of contract? When contract is part of the economic constitution of society it is evident its legal system must take cognisance of contract; for the observance of contract then affects its existence vitally. But when contract between individuals is no longer part of the economic constitution of things such "contract" ceases to have any social importance as to its performance or non-performance. "Contract" will then be understood to be a purely private agreement. The community does not ask Peter to trust Paul; he does it on his own responsibility, and he has no right to come, whining to the delegated authorities of the community for redress if Paul proves untrustworthy, or to expect the community to waste resources in keeping up machinery for the purpose of deciding disputes between them, with the chances, after all is done and under the most favourable circumstances, of as frequently arriving at a wrong as at a right decision. The principle once established that contract rests solely upon Honour; that another agreement, tacit or avowed, verbal or written, that I choose to enter into with another man, has no law to back it – must inevitably have a moral effect in the long-run of the most beneficial kind. Civil action concerned with contract being thus entirely anti-Socialistic in principle, its abolition ought, we insist, to be one of the first measures of that people's state whose final aim is to supersede the state itself by the Society.

To turn now to the case of civil action which does not refer to "contract," and which probably to many people nursed under current prejudices will seem of vital importance to maintain the action for libel or slander, to wit. This "action" is supposed necessary to the vindication of personal character against attack. In the first place, the law relating to libel is double-barrelled, so to speak: it is criminal as well as civil. But in referring to it I may as well say at once that I have included both aspects of it. The ambiguous nature of its rationale is pretty clearly indicated by the doubt hanging over it as to whether it is directed against false imputations or any imputations whatever, true or false. The law, a far as we understand, technically covers both; but the principle of farthing damages and no costs conveniently obviates the constant display of the fulness of its absurdity.

No greater or more unwarrantable restriction on freedom of speech or writing is, to our thinking, conceivable than this law of libel and slander. We beg the reader to put aside his prejudices for a moment, and tell us whether it does not bear the most unmistakable impress of a corrupt society which it is possible to have. The law of libel, look at it what way one will, seems to be expressly designed to protect the acute rogue from the most legitimate consequences of his roguery. Vindicating character, forsooth, in proceedings for libel! Bah! Mr. Belt vindicated his character in this manner, got swinging damages, and a few months afterwards a jury convicted him of a more heinous offence than that originally alleged against him. Every man of the world knows that the successful issue of an action or a prosecution for libel does not mean the clearing of the plaintiff or prosecutor's character morally. More often than not it merely means that he is a clever rascal rather than a stupid one, or that he has got a clever counsel to represent him. The real raison d'etre of the law of libel in our hypocritical, hollow class-society is, as already hinted, written on its face: it is a stockade to protect rogues, and behind which every dirty scoundrel can sneak. The "privileged" classes know that their characters in many cases "will not bear investigation," to use the familiar phrase – "shady" transactions in business with neighbours' pockets; "shady" transactions out of business with neighbours' wives. What man of social position – above all, what self-made man – does not owe his position, at some point or other of his career, to something that, were it exposed to the light. of day, would constitute a libel for which, in the chicanery of law, he could obtain a verdict with heavy damages against the exposer? This explains the cold shiver with which the proposal to abolish all legal "protection of character" (sic!) is greeted by the average sensible man of business. His way of looking at things naturally extends itself to people who have no personal motives to influence them: the tendrils of a sentiment having their root in class corruption ramify far and wide. What every Socialist ought to stand by is perfect freedom of speech and writing so far as personal character is concerned. The Socialist is the last person who ought to form harsh judgements of, or hardly deal with, individuals for their failings but he ought nevertheless to insist that every man has a right – the advisability or charity of doing so resting with himself – that he has a right, we say, to make known his opinion concerning any other man, be it good or bad, just or unjust, in any way he pleases. We all know that our present class-society – with its commercial and its social rottenness – could not stand for a month the wholesome douche which would result from the withdrawal of the legal protection behind which successful rascaldom skulks, at the first scent of danger discharging its "solicitor's letter" threatening "proceedings."

I have been accused in some quarters of intolerance, because, forsooth, I think that children and ignorant and weak-minded persons (so long as such exist) ought to be protected by society from the ravings of a certain class of dogmatic theologians, even if necessary to the placing of such theologians under physical restraint. Probably the same persons who profess such unbounded Laissez faire on current lines, and whose Whig ideas of "toleration" are so shocked at, the bare notion of any repression of opinion or free speech, even when it means the terrorising or susceptible imaginations to the point of insanity, would evince at the notion of the right of free speech being extended to the opinion that they are morally undesirable persons. The bourgeois Radical finds his free-expression-of-opinion principles begin to fit him rather tight here. He finds it is surely most unjust that such an abominable lie should be circulated about him with impunity, when no one that knows him can have the slightest suspicion but that he is a most desirable person – especially morally. Free speech, my friend! Your adversary merely expresses an opinion concerning your actions or your motives. It is open to you to say he is wrong, and to show reason for believing that not you but he is the undesirable person for that matter. What more do you want? Is it "the part" of a magnanimous mind secure in a sense of its own rectitude to wish to persecute the misguided wretch who presumes to express an opinion derogatory therefrom? Of course, given a law of libel we are well aware an individual may find himself handicapped in not availing himself of it, since in the event of a direct attack on his character, if he does not "clear" (?) himself, public opinion will allow the case against him to go by default; but this is no argument for the maintenance of the system. What I contend for is the right of every man to impeach my character, if he cares to, to the top of his bent, provided I have the same right as regards his. The abolition of legal restraints in free criticism of character, it is true, might lead at the outset to a prolific crop of mere malicious slanders. Like a new toy such criticism might at first be a constant recreation with some people. But it is easy to see that this would cure itself in a very short time. Assuming, as will probably be urged, that every man having a grudge against another would instantly proceed to circulate the statement that he had robbed his aged father, and that his untiring attentions at the bedside of his sick wife were to be explained by the fact that he was engaged in administering digitalis in small doses, or that his solicitude for his niece's welfare masked incestuous relations, how long would it be before every sane person had ceased to heed any allegation made respecting another without corroborative evidence? Things having reached this stage how much longer would it be before the fashion of making false allegations had died out? Even now, who heeds the whispered insinuations made at election times about the character of rival candidates; or the many suspicions places in which Mr. Gladstone or any other public man is said to have been seen. The very fact of the existence of a law against slander keeps the practice of slander alive by giving evil insinuation a sting much to the detriment of the man against whom they are groundless. The slanderer can always plead the terror of the law in excuse for not giving definite shape to his dark hints. He "could an' if he would" dilate upon certain things he knows, but prudence compels him to be silent as to any specific charge.

The argument is commonly used, that were "legal redress" for libel and slander removed, physical force would be employed and breaches of the peace ensue. We hardly think the really calumniated would so conspicuously put themselves in the wrong. The employment of physical force against the "allegator" is often strong presumptive evidence of the truth of the allegation. An assault is no answer to a charge –

Und könnt' ich sie zusammen schmeissen

Könnt' ich sie doch nicht Lügner heissen.[1]

Any scoundrel can commit an assault or get one committed for him, and the legitimate inference is that the intention of committing the assault was only the last resort of an ignoble mind unable to rebut the charge. In any case, personal violence is a criminal offence, to be dealt with as such. The baselessness in reason and inutility in practice, so far as honest men are concerned, of laws against libel is so plain, in short, that they may be taken as the most crucial illustration of the truth with which we started, that they exist, like all civil law, firstly, for the sake of the legal class; and secondly, for the benefit of the many doubtful personages that throng the commercial, political, and "society" worlds, but whom it is not convenient to have exposed. They are emphatically class laws.

E. Belfort Bax

## Notes

1. "And if I could beat them up, I still couldn't call them liars.

# Appendix

## Notes on Universal History from a Socialist Standpoint

From The Religion of Socialism, pp.164-177.

I

THE inability referred to in the text, to envisage the past otherwise than with the atmosphere of the present, is apparent in all popular notions of past ages. Exceedingly funny is the unsuspecting guilelessness with which the ordinary politician talks of the English Parliament as having been instituted by Simon de Montfort, as though Simon's war-council were an institution essentially the same, after all, as our House of Commons; or of the compact wrung, for their own purposes, by a band of semi-independent barons, or territorial potentates, from their feudal overlord, called Magna Charta, with the, unquestioning belief that he is referring to a great popular "measure" similar in kind to Mr. Gladstone's latest Franchise Act only "more so". These belong to a class of historical misconceptions for which language is largely responsible. The same name is used for the most diverse things, simply because there is a thread of historical continuity running through them. This continuity between the things becomes, in popular conception, confounded with likeness, or even identity. The term "parliament" or "Commons Assembly" being used both for the casual assembling of feudal estates, for the purpose of supplying their feudal superior with the means of carrying on a war, and also for the modern "representative" institutions of constitutional government, has led the ordinary mind to conceive the two things as closely connected, if not identical; whereas, of course, there is hardly an appreciable point in common between them. The same class of misconception attaches to the words "money," "merchant," "usury," "trade," etc. The ordinary newspaper-reading intellect has little notion that these words, in past periods of the world's history, when economical conditions were totally unlike the present, connote different things to what they do to-day. The popular conceptions of ancient history and quasi-history, especially the Bible, are of course the most flagrant illustrations of what we speak of: these sometimes take a comical form, such as the Anglo-Israel craze. In this case of course there is the additional fact that the story of the rise and fall of the Jewish state is viewed through the distorting lenses of a theology which has passed through a long development, and been fundamentally modified several times, before arriving at that perfect adaptability to the needs of middle-class Philistinism presented in orthodox Protestant Christianity. The special unhistorical twist for which this theology is responsible is, we may mention, often quite as noticeable in those who reject it – should they happen to be persons without much culture, such as the average Secularist lecturer, – as in those who accept it. An instance of this latter is afforded by what until quite recently passed for the "Bible-smashers" special text-book, and which we were all brought up to regard as the abomination of desolation, – albeit, to-day its theology is suggestive of little more, barring its specially eighteenth century characteristics, than the discourse of a mild Unitarian divine with evangelical leanings, – to wit, Paine's Age of Reason, – and more or less of all writings of which that is the type. The Bible, to the critical student of history, contain the indications of a growth of a few loosely connected Phoenenician or Canaanitish tribes of nomads into a coherent "people," and thence into a little state; the ancestral and tribal cults gradually succumbing to the civic or national cult which became identified with the worship of Jaho or Yahveh, established at Jerusalem, the "sacred" city; the struggle of this cult to maintain its supremacy over the other indigenous religions as well as over those imported

132

from without; its varying success until curiously enough at became associated with the great introspective ethical movement of the prophets, and merged finally into the later Judaism; the whole, with the exception, perhaps, of the last point named, in which the special race individuality comes into play, forming simply a story a thousand times repeated in all essential features in early ages, wherever a "people" has developed: civilisation of any kind. But by the "uncritical" man, whether his bias be theological or anti-theological, the Bible, in its present form, is regarded pretty much as the work of good or bad individual authors, and the whole narrative portion much as the history of a modern state, the prominent actors in which are to be respectively praised or blamed as though they were Lord Salisburys or Mr. Gladstones. It is little suspected that the nearest analogue to-day to the Hebrews in their legendary period is to be found in the tribes of the Lebanon or the Soudan. Again, what orthodox English Nonconformist has any suspicion that the Founder of Christianity was other than a kind of sublimated Samuel Morley, in appropriate costume. Could the messianic prophet of the first century, lying hidden beneath the mythical "Jesus," revisit the "glimpses of the moon" in mufti, and give his impressions of "the young man preparing for the ministry " it would be certainly edifying. Only the pen of Heine could have given us a suggestion of the result.

The inability of man to interpret the past otherwise than in terms of the world in which he lives has been till the present century universal. Albrecht Dürer paints his Virgin and Apostles as the maiden and burghers of a medieval German town. So with all the other painters of the Middle Ages. In Shakespeare's "historical plays" the characters live and speak in the world of the sixteenth century. Racine, it has been said, introduced the "manners of Versailles to the camp of Aulis." The suspicion that contemporary manners and customs or at least contemporary sentiment and ethics, did ever not prevail has first seriously dawned upon mankind in the nineteenth century. The part cause and part consequence of this flash of insight has been modern "critical" history and "realistic" art. But it is as yet mainly the property of the literary class. To the lack of the historical sentiment is largely due the objection sometimes expressed respecting Socialism on the score of certain a priori view on "Human Nature." The man whose sole intellectual stock-in-trade consists in so-called "common sense" (that commodity which is, when highly developed, so very difficult to distinguish from its opposite) finds it even harder to conceive the future save in terms of the present than he does the past. Such a man will sometimes boldly assure you that certain things are opposed to "human nature," the "human nature" he has in his mind being his own, his son's, his next door neighbour's, his wife's, and marriageable daughter's nature. Human nature of course to the student of anthropology and history implies something which has been modified, to a virtually indefinite extent, in the past before it attained the sublimity of smug self-satisfaction expressed in British common sense, and will be still further indefinitely modified in the time that is to come, after British common sense shall have gone to its last rest. "As it was in the beginning is now and ever shall be" may be a very good motto for the bourgeois Philistine, for whom both past and future are merely a reduplicated present; but it won't pass muster with any one ungifted with the sound "common sense" and comprehensive ignorance of that individual.

II

The stage of development of Humanity as a whole must be gauged by the outer edge, so to speak, of progress that is, by the most advanced indications in the most advanced people at the period; it is in them that humanity is for the nonce most fully embodied and realised. They alone give the tone to all the rest.

For instance, until about the sixth century the Oriental monarchies represented this "human spirit" (to employ a Germanism), the Aryan races being far behind them. The torch then passed on to South Eastern Europe, which became the head-quarters of advancing human energy. In the Middle Ages the ancestors of the modern races of Western Europe embodied the active principle of human progress, etc. When once the particular stage has been reached and passed by the races in the van of progress – although to attain it they may have required a long and arduous development – it is henceforth achieved for all progressive races. The complete evolution which led up to it having once been passed through in its entirety by the highest group of races at the time being, can be attained by all less advanced races without passing through the same development. Thus the economic condition of Western Europe to-day has implied a development of four hundred years from medieval conditions. Yet this does not mean that backward races, in which the level of production corresponds to that of the Middle Ages with us, will require at this date to wait four hundred years before they reach the present condition of Western Europe. They may easily attain it in ten years. Russia, for instance, affords an illustration of this. Where but yesterday mediaeval methods of individualist production prevailed, to-day we see the great industry in its rankest growth. The same with the intellectual side of things. The most advanced thought of Western Europe subsists there side by aide with the most archaic superstition. Yet with these facts before their eyes, writers, who ought to know better, base arguments respecting the future on the relative backwardness of Russia at the present moment! The most advanced races, those in which the genius humunitatis is embodied at the time, workout a development vicariously, so to say, for the rest, who merely adopt its result. These latter may then easily take the lead in progress (start a new development of their own) while their superiors of yesterday fall into the background. This has been persistently the case throughout history.

Historic evolution, though one movement, is not the movement of one people or society, but a movement which passes through and uses up or exhausts, so to say, whole races one after the other. Indeed, the races touched by the breath of the movement of history, while receiving the seal of everlasting life in one sense, that is, as embodying a moment of historic evolution, receive the seal of death in another, that is, as actually existent races. The African savage untouched by civilisation lives on to-day as he was in Pliny's time, and as he might be two thousand years hence, so far as internal causes of decay are concerned. But what of the nations of Asia Minor, the Cilicians, the Lydians, the Carians, etc.? What of the Phoenicians, the Assyrians, the Hittites? Or, for that matter, what of the classical nations of Greece and Italy themselves, who can hardly be said to survive in their modern representatives? Each race that is drawn into the evolution of human society brings with it, besides its own grade of development, its own ethnical character, that is, the character it has had impressed upon it by climatic, topographical, and other considerations. This is one of the cardinal difficulties in an appreciation of history. Another difficulty is in the many-sided nature of human development. Although unquestionably the domestic and economical aspects of human affairs are the fundamental aspects – although industrial development is their foundation – yet social development is not purely industrial, but political, imaginative, religious, ethical, in addition. Were, for example, the historical order, the exact counterpart of the logical and were the development, a purely economical one taking place in one continuous society, we should find something like the logical process presented. But in the real process of history a particular aspect may be accelerated, retarded, or hold in solution at any stage. Archaic, domestic, and economic forms are preserved in religious beliefs and observances, etc.

136

# III

The best illustration of the "people" stage of social evolution is to be found in the Germanic tribes as they first appear in history, the Catti, the Suevi, the Allemanni, the Rutuli, etc., as described by Tacitus and later writers. The word "thiud," meaning people, enters into many of the names of Gothic chiefs and kings, e.g., Theodoric, Theobald, etc. The tract of land occupied by the "people" was the mark. Primitive Communism prevailed amongst them in the time of Tacitus, but the constant state of internecine war, and the tendency to rally round and exalt the victorious leader, betokened a ripeness for civilisation, which is further indicated by the tendency to acquire slaves, etc. For another instance of the "people" the reader may be referred to the early history of the Hebrew race. "What there was of permanent official authority," says Professor Wellhausen (Encyc. Brit., 9th ed" art. Israel), "lay in the hands of the elders and heads of houses; in time of war they commanded each his own household force, in peace they dispensed justice each within his own circle." And again, "actual and legal existence, in the modern sense, was predicable only of each of the many clans: the unity of the nation was realised in the first instance only through its religion." Herodotus is a rich mine for indications of the "people" stage. Among modern analogies may be mentioned the Kurdish tribes, the Arab, and other tribes of the Soudan, etc. It is, however, I think, important to remember what has been hinted in the text; that modern instances of primitive, social, and intellectual conditions can only with safety he regarded as a more or less close approach to those conditions of the historical races which obtained in early ages, and not as some writers, insist as necessarily identical with them. Similarly the modern anthropoid ape, though undoubtedly presenting in structure and habits a close analogy with the ape-like ancestor of man, is not regarded by naturalists as reproducing identically such ancestor. Just as species have become fixed it seems likely that races have become fixed. The very fact of the capacity for development or progress in the "culture-races" would seem to imply elements in them which from the earliest stages must have differentiated them from those "nature-races," where no such capacity exists.

## IV

The "city" was a system of families, gentes, and tribes, each with a special organisation of its own united together primarily for objects of production and defence, though descent from a common ancestor was always assumed for religious purposes. Every house had its domestic altar for its family divinities, every division of the city its temple or altar for the special clan or tribe dwelling within it, while the city itself possessed a central fanes, the largest and most, richly appointed of all for the worship of the city divinity. The city then was a system of separate governments as it was a system of separate religions, united together under one central government and religion. But it was not in its earlier stages a state in the full sense of the word. The political had not as yet become completely differentiated from the religious and social. At first the whole society was the state as the whole society was the church. The governing body was not external to the governed as it is to-day. The head of every family was an integral part of the governing power, as he was of the religious worship.

"Cité et ville n'étaient pas des mots anonymes chez les anciens. La cité était l'association religieuse et politique des familles et des tribus; la ville était le lieu de reunion, le domicile et surtout le sanctuaire de cette association." (La Cité Antique, p.155).

138

"Ainsi, la cité n'est pas un assemblage d'individus; c'est une confederation de plusieurs groupes qui étaient constitués avant elle, et qu'elle laisse subsister. On voit dans les orateurs attiques que chaque Athenien fait partie à la fois de quatre sociétés distinctes; il est membre d'une famille, d'une phratrie, al'une tribu et d'une cité." (ibid., p.142)

The city, at first a simple burg, or fortified place, gradually developed its architecture, etc. As types of the ancient city may be taken Troy the focus of the great Homeric epic; Jerusalem, the focus of the Hebrew epic embodied in the Old Testament: and Thebes, the focus of one of the most important cycles of Greek legend. Curiously enough, according to the usual supposition, these clusters of stories (or certainly the first two) arose about the same time (the ninth century BC), and received their final form about the same time (the fifth century BC).

V

Ancient religion did not concern itself with the supernatural in the sense of a spiritual sphere above, and essentially distinct from nature. Its prayers were usually invocations by magical formulae, designed to compel the will of the occult or invisible agent to that of the invocator. That religion in the ancient, world connected itself with the belief in such occult, or in the common acceptation of the word, supernatural agents and powers goes without saying, seeing that the whole of nature was conceived as a system of animated beings. But its concern with this larger system of nature was always more or less indirect. It was primarily occupied with human relations – the relation of the individual with the society into which he entered, of the family with its gens, of the gens with its tribe, of the tribe with the people or city. The gods or supernatural agents when

139

they failed in their protection of the society which practised their cult were commonly insulted, and their images and altars thrown down. Religious sentiment did not centre in them, but in the community whose good or ill was supposed to lay in their power. The functions of the priesthood of course involved the knowledge of nature according to current conceptions – i.e., as a complex of occult agencies, in fact, as the more powerful counterpart of human society. A good picture of the ancient theocratic priest is given by Flaubert in Salaambo, in the person of Schahabarim.

The ancient religious cults might perhaps be classified as follows: first, probably both in order of time and importance, as attaching themselves directly to the society, the ancestral cults; and, secondly, the nature cults proper from amongst the indefinite number of which two stand out in respect both of the wideness, amounting almost to universality, of their diffusion, and of their significance – the Solar and the Phallic cult. The worship of the traditional founder of the clan, the tribe, the people, etc., respectively as divine, is the basis of the ancestral cults; the naive primitive personification of nature is the basis of the nature cults. Two of the most striking of natural phenomena to the early mind, are (1) the sun, the giver of light, heat, fruitfulness, the cause of the seasons, the bringer also of death, corruption, and devastation; and (2) the generative organs, the material symbol of social continuity. In the one early man saw the great principle of external or economic life and progress, upon which society so vitally depended – the fecundating power in nature; in the other the great internal principle of life and progress in society itself. Hence the apparently endless changes the mythologies and religions of antiquity ring upon these two themes; hence the variety of Solar gods and heroes – i.e., of personifications of different aspects of the sun's influence, noxious and beneficent, and the numberless Phallic divinities and symbols with which ancient religion abounds. Memories of older family and social forms doubtless also lingered on, and were perpetuated in

140

religious, rites and ceremonies, – a fact which no doubt enters largely into the explanation of the "sacred prostitution" of many ancient peoples. The custom or practice dictated by the social necessities of one age becomes the religious rite hallowed by tradition of another age, when its necessity has passed away and its meaning is forgotten, such meaning having become embodied in other customs and practices.

## VI

It must be borne in mind that production being carried on mainly by slaves, who formed part of the family of the citizen, there was practically no exploitation of labour under the form of "free-contract" such as is the key-stone of modern capitalism. The "rich man" of antiquity was of the nature of a hoarder of treasure. The notion of increasing this treasure by means of the process of circulation was almost entirely foreign to him. His idea was to preserve it intact, either in the shape of houses, furniture, slaves, etc., or in that of the precious metals which he would probably bury. This wealth did not create wealth, except occasionally in the form of simple and direct usury, for which, in most cases, the borrower had in the last resort to pay with his skin, by becoming the property or chattel-slave of the lender, thus terminating the transaction. The "rich man" added to his hoard of course when he could, but the addition was generally altogether independent of the existent hoard itself. Hence the wealth of the "rich man" was constantly at hand in a concrete shape to be directly appropriated. In the disturbances which occurred in some of the Greek cities, – e.g., Samos, between the rich and the poor, this hoarded wealth often changed hands in the lump, so to speak, two or three times. The poor citizens would rise and drive the rich out, and take possession of their wealth; the rich would subsequently return in force and retake their property.

141

## VII

There is one point in the trite parallel between the circumstances of the execution of Socrates and that of Jesus, which I am not aware has ever been noticed before. Long previous to the preaching of an introspective ethic by Socrates in Europe, the Hebrew prophets had preached an ethic and religion having the same tendency. After the exile a compromise was effected between their doctrine and the older national cultus, which took the form of Judaism, the poliadic or state divinity Yahveh being erected into the supernatural god of the universe, demanding a "religion of the heart," but his national character being preserved in the "chosen people" theory.

Like all compromises, this illogical position was eventually assailed. The creed of the prophets culminated in Jesus. The orthodox Jew sought to combine the spiritualistic individualism of the prophets with the old civic ideal of life, of the decay of which this individualism was the sign. Hence in the Palestine of the Christian era there were two streams of tendency, one drawing from the tradition of the prophets, and the other from that of the older priesthood. The founder of Christianity by taking his stand on inwardness, personal holiness, purity of heart, etc., and by his open contempt for the surviving symbols of the old political cultus, roused the not unnatural resentment of the citizens of Jerusalem, with whom the old sentiment was naturally strongest, and for whom the ancient city and temple were still "holy," and the sanctuary of the fathers; many of them, indeed, like the Sadducees, caring little for the later tendencies. The result was as at Athens, a conspiracy to be rid of the blasphemous radical. Thus alike in the crucifixion of Jesus, as in the death of Socrates we may see illustrated the conflict between the ancient communist ideal of devotion to the race, and the new individualist ideal of devotion to the soul, and to its non-natural source. In the "know thyself" of Socrates and "seek ye first his kingdom and his righteousness" of Jesus we have an expression of the same movement, mirrored on the one hand in the logical clearness of the Attic thinker, in the other in the dreamy, introspection of the Syrian mystic.

I may take this opportunity of remarking concerning the "community of goods" supposed to have been practised by some of the early Christian bodies, that this cannot be taken by any but the most superficial observer as implying any socialistic tendency as inherent in early Christianity. Like that of the later monkery it is perfectly obvious that the communistic mode of life was a mere accident. It was simply a means to another end that end being individual salvation. To avoid the distractions incident to ordinary life and affairs they were abandoned; the individual being hereby better able to concentrate his attention on his soul and "heavenly things." The ascetic motive of course came in as well; the mere self-sacrifice was in itself to certain extent an end.

## VIII

The exclusiveness of the ancient societies which the Roman Empire and the new ethics combined to break down is almost inconceivable to-day. Each division of the politico-social hierarchy, as already pointed out, was more or less of a closed corporation, a masonic guild, the members of which were bound to each other by the closest of ties, but by ties which had no validity beyond that division. Special religious forms bound a man to his family, others to his clan, others to his tribe, others again to his city, others yet again through them generally of a less intimate and sacred character to the group of cities (the country or kingdom) to which he belonged. There, however, all duty, all sentiment of a common humanity came to an abrupt ending.

143

Beyond the state as federated group of cities, as kingdom or empire, all were Gentiles, outer barbarians, heathen. Such was the inseparability of morality and religion from politics, that a human being outside the political boundary was altogether outside the pale of human relations. The consequence of this negative attitude of the ancient racial morality towards the outer world was rich in consequences – warfare and slavery directly flowed from it. The conquering power had no duties towards the conquered, and hence its one idea was to utilise them in the interest of its own commonwealth, into which they were therefore introduced. The original political exclusiveness thus paved the way to a social exclusiveness, to the existence of a population within the commonwealth towards which its members owed no duties, and which of course had no rights. Exclusiveness, political and social, may be described as the negative element in the system of the ancient world, to the development of which it was indeed necessary, but which, nevertheless, proclaimed its inevitable fall in the very fact of that development – ancient society was strangled by its exclusiveness.

IX

The two streams, the one traceable to the customs and superstitions of the German tribes, and the other to the Church of the decaying Roman Empire, is clearly visible in the social and religious system of the Middle Ages. Feudalism was as entirely the offspring of the former as Monasticism was of the latter. The "hale young knight," whose "hand was in his country's right, whose heart was in his lady's bower," was as lineally descended from the German of Tacitus, who followed his chief to battle, as the "religious recluse" was from the monks of the Thebaid. Throughout the Middle Ages we can see the true streams of tendency – sometimes uniting, sometimes in conflict. It is quite clear that the acceptance of Christianity by the German peoples could have been little more than nominal. How could the German in the full vigour of tribal life really embrace a religion which placed the highest object of existence in submissive suffering, to purify the individual soul, as against that which the early world with one consent regarded as summing up the whole duty of man, namely, fighting and working for the political body? And in fact lie did not accept it more than nominally. Duty, fealty to the feudal superior, as representing the community, continued for ages to be the mainspring of his life. Even with the monk, as a general rule, it was the welfare of his order which was uppermost in his thoughts rather than his own personal salvation, as Carlyle has remarked in Past and Present, and this, notwithstanding that the genesis of Monasticism itself is traceable to a totally opposite sentiment.

## X

The Protestant notion of "reverence" that is, of a special sanctimonious bearing towards things religious, is a direct offspring of that extreme separation of religion from daily life which Protestant:, and above all Puritan, Christianity represents. It is nearly certain that the early Christians did not know it, and that their love-feasts were not "prayer-meetings." They were too near to Paganism with its joyous festivals and its conception of a living intercourse between gods and men, to have appreciated the morose priggishness involved in the "reverential attitude of mind" which is de rigeur with Protestantism. A religion which really interpenetrates life does not require the "reverential" pose. Homo sum, et nil humani a me alienum puto. Levity is a side of human nature, and a religion that eschews levity by that very fact signs its own death-warrant as a living power among men. I should observe in spite of what has just been said, that Christianity, without doubt, contained from the first the germ of this sentiment, although it may not have manifested itself immediately; British Sabbatarism is the hideous abortion it has brought forth.

www.ingramcontent.com/pod-product-compliance
Lightning Source LLC
Chambersburg PA
CBHW070141290526
45789CB00002B/577